SIMPLY THE BEST

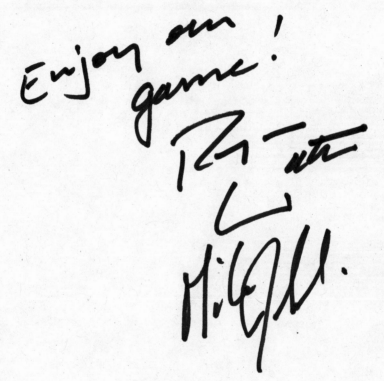

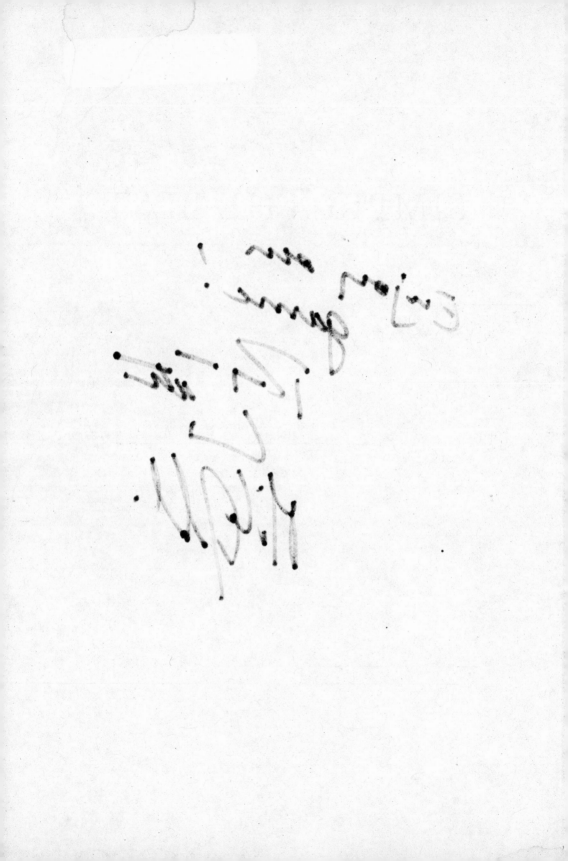

SIMPLY THE BEST

Players on Performance

Mike Johnston and Ryan Walter

VICTORIA • VANCOUVER • CALGARY

Heritage House Publishing Company Ltd.   Heritage House Publishing Company Ltd.
#108 – 17665 66A Avenue   PO Box 468
Surrey, BC V3S 2A7   Custer, WA
www.heritagehouse.ca   98240-0468

Library and Archives Canada Cataloguing in Publication
Johnston, Mike, 1957–

Simply the best: players on performance/Mike Johnston and Ryan Walter.

ISBN 978-1-894974-24-0

1. Hockey. 2. Hockey players. I. Walter, Ryan, 1958–   II. Title.

GV847.J64 2007   796.962   C2007-906185-0

Library of Congress Control Number: 2007931922

Cover design: Frances Hunter
Book layout: Darlene Nickull
Cover photo of Joe Sakic and Scott Niedermayer courtesy of Hockey Canada
Interior photos courtesy of Hockey Canada, except for Trevor Linden photographs, courtesy of Jeff Vinnick/Vancouver Canucks

Printed in Canada

Heritage House acknowledges the financial support for its publishing program from the Government of Canada through the Book Publishing Industry Development Program (BPIDP), Canada Council for the Arts, and the province of British Columbia through the British Columbia Arts Council and the Book Publishing Tax Credit.

The Canada Council | Le Conseil des Arts
for the Arts | du Canada

BRITISH COLUMBIA
ARTS COUNCIL
Supported by the Province of British Columbia

This book was produced on 100% post-consumer recycled paper, processed chlorine free and printed with vegetable-based dyes.

"In life and especially in a game, everything comes down to how players handle the few decisive seconds in a critical situation."
—George Kingston

Contents

Foreword

Mike Johnston is a career coach, and I was a player in the NHL from 1978 to 1993, yet over all those seasons our paths never crossed, even though the hockey world is a very small one. It wasn't until Mike, Myrna, and their children moved to Vancouver, BC, that our paths collided.

Out of our many conversations came a synergistic desire to explore the depths of coaching and high performance. We decided that the self-help and high-performance literature offered very little from the best athletes in the world and the experts who coach them. We started in the dressing room, interviewing 12 top coaches. *Simply the Best: Insights and Strategies from Great Hockey Coaches* was so successful and well received that we are now pleased to bring you our second book. While the first book focused on how professional coaches create a success culture for their players, our second, *Simply the Best: Players on Performance*, digs deeply into how the best in the world prepare, achieve, lead and like to be led.

The body of this work is about performing at the highest level. We wanted to interview players who struggle with issues, like you do, and yet have found simple, practical, real ways to become simply the best! Mike and I also wanted to uncover their ideas and experiences around how best to lead a dressing room from the inside out. Our athletes have provided us with amazing insights.

Finally, Mike and I wanted these players to shed light on the ways that coaches have gotten the best out of them over the years. In our first book, we asked some of the best coaches in professional hockey to give us their answers on how to get the most out of players. In the following pages, we ask some of the best athletes in the world how coaches have inspired their best performances.

We hope the words, ideas, and stories of these spectacular athletes and amazing people will simply inspire your best!

On behalf of my teammates, Jennifer, Myrna, and Mike,

Sidney Crosby

Sidney Crosby ("Sid the Kid"), the pride of Cole Harbour, Nova Scotia, has been hailed by the Great One as the *next* Great One. Crosby's winning ways started early. His 18 points in five games led the Midget AAA Dartmouth Subways to the national championship where he was awarded Most Valuable Player and Top Scorer honours. Next, he helped Minnesota's Shattuck–St. Mary's Sabres reach the US National Championship in 2002–03. From there, Sidney was selected first overall in the midget draft by the Rimouski Océanic of the Quebec Major Junior Hockey League (QMJHL), where he started the 2003–04 season with two consecutive Player of the Week awards, winning the honour four more times that season. He was named Player of the Month three times, and CHL Player of the Week three times, as well as Player of the Year, Top Rookie, and Top Scorer by the end of the 2003–04 season—the first QMJHL player to win all three at once. Crosby again won the Player of the Year and Top Scorer awards the following season, as well as the Most Valuable Player and Personality of the Year awards (both of which he had also won in 2004), and he added Best Professional Prospect and Playoff

MVP to his resume. It came as no surprise when the Pittsburgh Penguins drafted Crosby first overall in what came to be known as the "Sidney Crosby Sweepstakes of 2005."

In 2005–06, Crosby's first NHL season, the records started shattering. Crosby played the first part of his rookie season alongside "Super Mario" Lemieux and immediately broke two of Lemieux's franchise records: most assists and most points scored by a rookie. Lemieux retired mid-season, and Crosby was appointed an alternate captain. He finished the 2005–06 season on the NHL All-Star Rookie team and was runner-up to Alexander Ovechkin for Rookie of the Year. He was also sixth in the NHL scoring race and seventh in assists, and the youngest player and seventh rookie in the history of the NHL to score 100 points in a single season.

In 2006–07, his second NHL season, Crosby became the seventh player in NHL history to win the Hart Trophy, Art Ross Trophy, and Lester B. Pearson Award concurrently. He also holds a slew of youngest-ever NHL records, including the youngest player to:

- score 100 points in a season
- score 200 career points
- tally 2 consecutive 100 point seasons
- be voted to the NHL All-Star Game
- be named captain
- win the Lester B. Pearson Award
- be named to the First All-Star Team
- win the Art Ross Trophy, which made Sidney Crosby the youngest (and only teenaged) scoring champion in any major North American professional sport.

Crosby's youngest-ever records extend to his international play. On December 28, 2003, 16-year-old Sidney became the youngest player ever to score a goal for Team Canada at the World Junior Championships. He helped Team Canada win silver at the 2004 World Junior Championships, and a gold medal in 2005. Crosby was named a Team Canada alternate captain at the World Championships in 2006, and by the tournament's end was named to the All-Star Team. In addition, he was proclaimed Best Forward and was the youngest World Championship player ever to be named the tournament's Leading Scorer.

Although he can be seen in everything from television commercials to *GQ* magazine, was nominated as a candidate for *Time* magazine's 100 Most Influential People of 2007 and has designed his own clothing line, Sidney Crosby still returns every summer to Nova Scotia and the people who claim him as their own.

The Interview

How important is leadership on your team?

It's important! You can never have too many leaders. If you want to win, it is absolutely necessary. You need to have people who are going to step up in key situations. Those guys make the difference, and the more leaders you have, the better off you are. I don't believe there is only one way to lead. Using any way you can to get your team to follow is the sign of good leadership. Personally, I prefer not to have to say as much, and just go out there and lead by what I do.

You have been made captain at a young age. What has that experience been like and what different dynamics does this create within the team?

I've only been a captain for a short time, but I don't feel the pressure of having to do it all myself. Many of the older guys on our team have really helped me carry the load. Being captain hasn't really changed things much. I have always tried to be responsible and accountable. There will always be pressure on and off the ice, but it is something I am comfortable with, and I am lucky to have great teammates to help me with this new challenge.

How have coaches gotten the best out of you personally?

It has always been when they have allowed for creativity. Especially as an offensive player, it is always nice to be given the okay to be creative and make mistakes, but be allowed to push yourself. I like the coach to be upfront and honest with me. Obviously, certain coaches have to push certain buttons, but some of this message needs to come from teammates also.

How much of motivating the player is the coach's job, and how much needs to come more from the player's initiative?

It is mostly up to the players, if they can, to motivate themselves. There are times when we all need an extra push, but it definitely needs to start from within. If you have a strong core of players in the room, most of the time they can send the wake-up call instead of the coach always having to. I think a coach understands that at certain times the wake-up call is going to be needed, but hopefully not a lot. But a coach shouldn't be afraid of doing it, because sometimes this message has to be delivered. The way I like a coach to communicate with me depends a lot on the situation. Sometimes I need a push, and other times support, or a pat. Too much of either does not usually work.

What does a winning environment feel like?

It is a very upbeat, energetic feeling. Everyone wants to get better, and nobody accepts losing. It's an atmosphere; it's a frame of mind. It starts with everyone, the training staff and the head office staff; it's the mentality of everyone and it carries right into the dressing room with the players. If everyone shares this mentality, they care about all the details of every job that they do, whether it's a trainer taking pride in making sure that the room is clean or making sure that the skates are sharp and the equipment's ready. If they take pride in that job, I think that's contagious, and so the players have to take pride in what they do. If every player takes pride in his job, then it creates that winning atmosphere.

What motivates or drives you? Did you always have that drive as a youngster playing hockey?

Yes. I think winning motivates me. I also really enjoy being part of a team; I've always enjoyed team sports more than individual sports. I like that feeling of knowing that everyone's pulling hard to reach one common goal. Whether you're a young player at a Christmas hockey tournament or in the NHL trying to win a Stanley Cup, that feeling remains constant. You are working together to achieve a common goal. In hockey or in the business world or in school, wherever it is, everyone works hard for something, and it's rewarding to achieve those goals.

How do you prepare for your best games? What are the keys to your preparation?

I don't think that there is one certain way I prepare. I have always been excited by the opportunity to play in a big game. I'm excited because I know the opportunity to win or be a part of something is there, but there is also a little bit of the fear of losing, so at the same time you have to find the right balance and be able to control your emotions. Some guys are full of energy and some guys are quiet and focused. I always try to find somewhere in between, where you have a frame of mind that is ready to go, but is also optimistic and energetic about the opportunity to do something well.

Mental toughness seems to be such an important part of your game. How did this come about for you?

I think mental toughness is just pure experience. You find ways to channel your emotion. For some guys it's easier than others. For my game, I need to be emotional. When the energy's not there, when the passion is gone, I don't think that I'll ever be the same player. The passion and emotion have to be there. It's a matter of channelling it, and I'm still learning how to do that. Just because you get to the NHL doesn't mean that you stop learning. For some guys that's easier than for others. I believe that I have to play with a bit of an edge, and that just comes from wanting to compete and wanting the puck and wanting to be involved.

My mental toughness came from being competitive and by trying to learn as much as possible from each experience. Everyone has their own way of dealing with adversity. For me, it was through learning how to approach things and being properly prepared.

You have had to make some adjustments dealing with adversity. Have you thought about what adjustments you have had to make being under the pressure of not only playing in the NHL, but also of being an NHL star?

You have to learn how to deal with it. The biggest thing is that when you look at adversity, expectations come to mind. You go through tough points winning and losing, whether it's individually or as a team. You learn things through adversity. You learn about yourself. You learn about your teammates. You go through tough times, and hopefully you don't have to go through those tough times again, but if you do, you're ready for it and know that there is light at the end of the tunnel. Adversity is just something that you get better at dealing with as you go through it. Hopefully you don't have to face too much of it, but the best way to deal with it is to see how you react to it when the time comes.

Talk to us about confidence. How do you get it and why does it go away?

A lot of my confidence comes from practice. If you commit yourself to practice, and you know that you've done all the right things and you're prepared, even sometimes if it doesn't work out, you know that you've done everything right. There are always going to be tough times in the season. That's going to happen no matter how good you are. When those tough times come, some people try to change everything, and sometimes that's the worst thing you can do. I think my confidence comes more from practising, knowing that I have worked on things and have improved things, and that when the time comes I'm going to be ready because I have prepared for it. I would say that preparation is a big part of confidence for me.

Describe a time when you were in a slump and not producing, and tell us how you broke out of it.

There have been times when things have just not gone my way, and I don't expect that to ever really change. The key is to stick with what has worked for you and make adjustments here and there, but definitely to not panic. If you stick to the basics, then things will turn around.

What were some of the setbacks that you experienced and how did you rebound from them?

We did not make the playoffs in my first year in the NHL, and I had never experienced that before. I tried to use that disappointment as motivation to never let it happen again.

What makes you hungry, Sidney? Why is being hungry so important to you?

When I think of being hungry, it comes back to passion. You have to want that challenge, and even when you're young, you have to want the puck. You don't want to hog it, but you have to want it. I can remember being 8, 9, 10 years old and wanting to win as badly as I do now. I don't know if I was different than other kids, but I think I have always had that competitive element that I'm sure a lot of kids have. You want to win and you want to be the best. I think that a lot of it comes down to passion.

In your experience so far, how important is it to have a team that is hungry?

You have to expect a lot of each other; that's just the way it is. You have to make each other better. A lot of times when you watch winning teams practise, you see each guy pushing the other. That comes back to the winning atmosphere and environment and everyone pulling the same way. That's how it works. Everyone's got to have the same goal.

You have mentioned that Steve Yzerman was your favourite player. Why was Stevie Y the player that you looked up to?

I just liked how he did everything. Obviously, Mario Lemieux and Wayne Gretzky were all of our heroes, with the highlight reels and the records and all that. Steve Yzerman was always right behind those guys. There were 10 or 15 years of either Mario or Wayne or Jaromir Jágr winning the scoring titles and setting the records, and Steve was kind of always third or fourth on the charts. I always admired the things he did. The way he led, blocking shots and playing at key times, whether it was to score a goal or to stop one. You could just see that he really had the respect of his teammates and was willing to do anything that it took to win. He really would show up in big games, and I admired that too. He was just someone who was complete. Even when I saw him in interviews, he seemed like himself. He didn't seem like anyone different, he was himself, and I really respected that too.

Was there something about the experience of minor hockey that sticks out for you?

I have nothing but great memories. It's even fun sometimes just to think about it. I was so fortunate to play on winning teams every year. We played in Provincials and Atlantics and all those types of tournaments. There are guys that I played with or against who are now either playing in the AHL or the NHL. You don't think about it at the time, but it's just fun to look back and remember those experiences. It was mostly the same group of kids in my first year and second year at every level of minor hockey growing up and it was fun to be around those kids. We all played either hockey or baseball together; it was a fun way to grow up, for sure.

Tiger Woods talks a lot about the influence that his father had on his game and on him as a person. How has your father influenced you and the game that you play?

He's definitely been there since day one, and really, he has been the one to teach me the lessons and educate me on everything that I know about hockey. I've always tried to learn from everyone, but his opinion is something that I have definitely paid attention to. Whether it was school or hockey or life in general, the biggest things I think I learned from my parents were to never take anything for granted, just be my best at anything that I did, and not to settle for doing something just for the sake of doing it. Those lessons have always stuck with me.

Was it difficult to balance school and hockey?

It was a bit tough at times, but it's easy to use school as an excuse. It can be done. If you really put the effort forth and really make your teachers aware that you're willing to make the effort, even though it might not always be totally on time, or you might have to wait until you get back and catch up (which is not always the most fun thing to do), if you really put your mind to it and manage your time right, it can be done. I think my parents had a big influence in that too. They didn't let things slide in the classroom as far as that was concerned. They made sure that if I wanted to play hockey, I had to take care of school too. I was always mad at my friends because they were getting notes to give to the teachers saying that they had hockey practice and couldn't do their homework. I remember asking for a few of those, but I wasn't lucky enough to get any.

You said if you could be in any other occupation outside of sport that you would be a firefighter. Why?

I think being a firefighter is something that requires you to be active. There is probably a little bit of pressure that comes with that, obviously. You have to save people's lives, and fighting a fire obviously brings risk into the job. The aspect of constantly having a new challenge attracts me, and I think firefighting is something I would enjoy doing. I think basically that this comes from being competitive. If I had to choose between being active in a job or sitting at a desk all day, I would much rather be active.

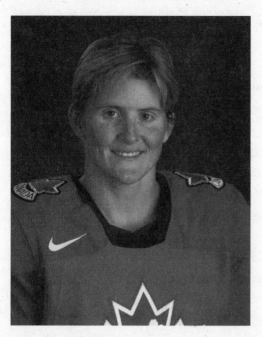

Hayley Wickenheiser

Perhaps no other name is as well known in Canadian women's hockey as Hayley Wickenheiser's. Cousin to late Montreal number-one overall draft pick Doug Wickenheiser, "High Chair Hayley" has been a Women's National Team player since the astounding age of 15, when she captured her first of seven World Championship gold medals in 1994, 1997, 1999, 2000, 2001, 2003, and 2007. She made the tournament All-Star Team in all of her World Championship appearances, including 2007, when she was also named top forward, leading scorer, and MVP. The native of Shaunavon, Saskatchewan, is the all-time leading scorer with Canada's National Women's Team, became an alternate captain in 2001 and was named captain in August 2006, a position she also held on Canada's National Women's Under-22 Team in 1998.

Hayley has amassed a dizzying array of awards on her way to competing at four separate Olympic Games. She was a member of Canada's silver-medal-winning women's hockey team at the 1998 Olympic Winter Games in Nagano, Japan. She then competed in the 2000 Olympic Summer Games as a member of Canada's softball team, becoming only the second Canadian woman to compete in both the summer and winter Olympics and the first to do so in team sports. Wickenheiser returned to hockey for the 2002 Olympic Winter Games in Salt Lake City, Utah, where she captured a gold medal and the MVP award for women's hockey. She then won yet another gold medal in Torino in 2006, along with tournament MVP and leading scorer, all the while playing with a broken wrist. She ranks first all time in Olympic scoring with 34 points.

Not content to merely dominate women's hockey, Hayley attended two Philadelphia Flyers rookie camps in 1998 and 1999 before signing with Salamat of the Finnish league in 2003, for whom she played parts of two seasons. In January 11, 2003, she became the first woman to score a goal in a men's professional hockey league.

Hayley has appeared on a children's television program with her son, Noah, had a children's book written about her (*Born to Play*), has conducted nationwide girls' hockey clinics and visited children in Rawanda. She is a role model in every sense of the word and a wonderful embodiment of her personal motto, "Excellence and Professionalism." Hayley Wickenheiser was awarded a doctor of laws degree from the University of Newfoundland in 2007.

The Interview

Who were the best leaders you ever played with and what made them the best?

Three names that come to mind are Stacey Wilson, France St. Louis, and Judy Diduck. They were leaders to me when I was a younger player, when leadership is really important, because they taught me what it took to win and how to be part of a winning team. The tradition and success we have with the Women's National Team is no coincidence. It goes back to the strong leaders and coaches. Shannon Miller, Danielle Sauvignon, Mel Davidson, Tim Bothwell, and Wally Kozak all excelled because of the preparation and passion they have for the game. I remember how passionate France St. Louis was. When I was a 15-year-old player, I watched her play and saw how passionate she was about the game, even when she was 35 years old. I remember what these coaches taught me and try to carry those traditions on and pass them on to the next group of players.

What were some other things they taught you?

I think just the sense of team that you have to have in order to win. You've got to buy in to whatever the team is trying to do. Everyone plays a role with our national team. We talk a lot about celebrating our small victories, whether it's a great pass by a defenceman, or a rush, or a save by the goaltender, and then validating everyone's spot on the team. We do a lot of things to accomplish that, like having a special defenceman for a day, or catering to the "D" for a day to make them feel special, or the coaches using video to motivate and help the players, or other different team-building things. I think more than that, when you get on the ice, you have to know that everybody is playing for each other. And you have to make sure good leadership is in place on the team.

How do players lead a dressing room?

I think there are a variety of ways. I've always been on teams where you have players who are sort of the outspoken ones who like to step up and speak. Then you have the players who keep the mood light with lots of joking around and are never at a loss for words. Finally, you have your quiet leaders and players who just get the job done. They don't need to say a lot; everybody feeds off the vibe that those players are giving. I think you need a good mix of these qualities, and you need a very safe atmosphere in the dressing room where everybody can go in and feel like, "Hey, I'm comfortable. I belong in this environment and I'm safe to speak my mind on whatever I feel." I think those are really key things for a team.

What are your strongest leadership qualities?

I tend to think of myself as someone who leads by example. I like to prepare as much as I can off the ice so that when I'm in a game situation, especially a big game, I am able to score that goal or make a play and get the job done. I'm not a very vocal leader in that regard, but I will step up and say things if they need to be said. I would consider myself a pretty intense player and person, so more than anything I think I lead by body language.

Did you perceive any difference when you played on a men's team?

I played boys' hockey growing up. Men and women are different in the dressing room. Men, I think, can take criticism better than women; they don't carry it with them. Sometimes if something is said, women can't just leave it on the ice; we have to drag it out and talk about it. By the same token, I think women listen better and take better direction than men or boys do. Women want to be told why, and men just want to be told how and what—"Just tell me what to do and I'll do it"—so I find that the leadership dynamic is different. You can have a much more direct approach with the men's team than you can with the women's team. This was certainly something that I noticed, and I almost respond better in a male environment, at times. It's just the type of player that I am, so it's an adjustment to the women's game when I go back.

Not everyone wears an "A" or a "C" or is set up in a position of leadership. How important have you found the glue guys or glue gals on the teams to be?

I've actually found on the teams I've played on that sometimes the players that wear the "A"s and "C"s aren't necessarily the real leaders. I think that is something that doesn't truly matter, but you do have a core group of players, whether it's three, six, or eight, who are important because they set the standard and direction you want your team to go in. If you have those players onside, they're connected with the rest of the players in the room in different ways. Usually you have your whole team if you have your key players in place.

What have you respected about the coaches that you've played for?

If I look back to Torino 2006 with our staff of Mel Davidson, Tim Bothwell, and Margot Page, I just think preparation is a huge word that stands out. It was not only the amount of video they did after every game, and the stats, and the preparation for each practice that I respected. In a centralized program you're responsible for mapping out your hockey schedule, your off-ice conditioning, your travelling—it's basically a pro team and the coaches have to do all that. They don't have a lot of extra staff helping in that way, so I found that they were extremely prepared. They were right on with what we needed to do to be successful as a team. They really identified the strengths and weaknesses of our group of players well and used that to make us a better team. In the past years, I think of 2002 with Danielle Sauvignon as head coach and the experience that Wally Kozak brings and his knowledge of the game in men's or women's hockey. There are not many guys that know their game like Wally does, just the technical ability that he had to help our team. And then there was

Danielle's ability. I think as a coach one key thing is you've got to step back and let your players just play and try not to over-coach. That was one thing that really stands out in my mind.

How did coaches get the best out of you?

I always found that I responded to coaches who were very straight up and honest with me, who just had a direct approach. If they didn't like something they would come and tell me, and if they wanted more they would challenge me. I think a coach who challenges you to be better, as well as a coach who gives you respect and speaks to you on an equal level, is a good thing for a player. As a player, you always respond to that.

How do you like to be communicated to? Is it the push that you talked about or the pat on the back that gets the best out of you?

I'm not really a player who needs a pat on the back, but every once in a while it's appreciated. It doesn't matter who you are, I think you always like to be appreciated when you do good work. Everybody likes a coach who gives them lots of ice time, so the more you're playing the more you usually like your coach, but definitely at times a kick in the butt helps if you're not performing well. Usually just a quiet challenge gets the most out of me. I don't need somebody to verbally confront me in front of the whole team; it's usually not effective.

How much of motivating the player is the coach's job, and how much should come from the player's initiative?

That's a good question. I believe that motivation comes from within, that you have to find ways within yourself to perform every night because a coach doesn't have time to worry about 20 players. Yes, there are times when a good conversation with the coach can clarify things and set your mind at ease, but ultimately as a player you have to find a way to get yourself ready for games night in and night out.

From a coaching and player point of view, would you agree that motivation comes from within but the coach or players can help to create an inspiring atmosphere?

I think the coach can really set the mood on a team, with what they say, their body language, how they approach the team, inspiring the team and saying the right thing at times when the team's not performing to turn it around, whether it's yell and scream or something calm and composed. I think there are so many different ways you can communicate. There's not one right way; there are times for everything, and a good coach really knows when to push those right buttons.

How did coaches or general managers build a winning environment in your past?

When I look at the tradition of excellence that Hockey Canada has had over my years on the team, I think the winning environment is due to the expectations that have passed from player to player who step into the Hockey Canada uniform from year to year, the accountability that we have to our team, the responsibility we have to prepare ourselves so that we're ready to go when we step out on the ice, the character and the class that we have to have to wear the uniform and handle ourselves around other people. It is the tradition of excellence. There's a real winning feeling we have within Hockey Canada, within the women's program. We believe we can win, and that's not really easy to explain. It's a real intangible, but as a player, when you come into an environment where you have everything you need to succeed and all you have to do is play, it's pretty easy to want to win.

Talk to us about the elements of a winning dressing room.

You need a comfortable atmosphere for sure. There are certain things that go on in a room: you've got to be able to challenge each other as teammates to get the best out of each other, and there has to be an open-door policy. Our coach, Mel Davidson, spoke a lot about kitchen-table talk, when you talk to each other as though you're sitting at home with your family around the kitchen table and keep what you say within the room. When you step on the ice, there's got to be a certain level of expectation that every day you're there to push each other to get better, and when somebody's not living up to those expectations, they need to be challenged to take it to the next level. You can never be complacent. You always need to raise the bar for each other.

What responsibility do we have as players to affect that winning environment?

Players can really influence it or hurt it. I believe it takes 20 players to create a winning environment, but only one to wreck it. One player with a bad attitude can really affect the team in a negative way, and it probably takes five or six players to make up for that. To keep that positive energy it's always a challenge to keep the negative away from the dressing room as much as possible. We always talk on our team about energy takers and energy givers. Some days you're not going to be your best when you show up at the rink or are on the ice, but trying to always give something positive no matter what is key to a successful team.

Give us some specific examples of an energy taker.

An energy taker makes selfish plays on the ice, selfish moves, and shows up late for a practice when she should be there an hour early. Showing up late for practice shows a lack of respect, as does not following the team rules. We have a set of team rules, and being late for the bus or something else is always one thing that has annoyed me as a player. An energy taker has negative body language if she's not getting the ice time that she wants, takes it out on others or is really down about it. I think wanting others to fail so that you get a chance to succeed is also energy taking. I've been around a lot of players, and you just feel that some players are hoping that you don't do well so that they'll get their chance. I think that's a natural feeling that we all have as humans at times, but there are ways that you can encourage others and still be able to do well yourself.

What are the specifics of the energy givers? What are some of the characteristics that people who read this book can attach to and say, "Oh, I can be that?"

It's nothing fancy. People who do their jobs are energy givers. Not everybody has the same role on a team. You might be a goal scorer, you might be a sixth defenceman, but everybody has a job to do. Usually every player on the team knows what every other player is doing, whether they're doing their job or not. I look at off-ice preparation: are you doing it conditioning-wise, warming up properly and cooling down properly? Do you have good body language? Are you being positive on the bench during games? Are you going up to players if it's a one-on-one situation in a practice, or any time, and saying, "Hey, that was a great pass," or "I liked how you played last night?" Those types of things can go a long way. I think just generally being a positive contributor to your team, always offering ways to get better and trying to become better as an individual, and helping the team get better sums up an energy giver.

What motivates you? What drives you? Did you always have this drive as a youngster?

I would say that I did. I started playing when I was about five. My dad built a rink in our backyard. He played old-timers hockey in a local rink in Shaunavon, Saskatchewan, and that's where I got my passion and really learned how to play the game. I watched *Hockey Night in Canada* and during the intermissions I would go out and skate. I loved the Oilers as a kid, so I would pretend that I was Messier or Gretzky. I would try to do the lay across the blue line like Gretzky or the shot off the wrong foot like Messier, all those things on the outdoor rink. I grew up playing with boys. I was the only girl on boys' teams probably until I was about 15, all the way to AAA Midget, so I went through a lot of situations where it wasn't very much fun to play as a kid. I think that if I didn't have the love for the game and the inner motivation and the drive to succeed I would have quit. There were times when parents would tell me, "You shouldn't play hockey; you should be figure skating." Or I'd have guys from the other team taking runs at me during the game and all sorts of things. I could go on and on, but really, my parents were there. They protected me from a lot of it, and they also at times asked, "Are you sure you want to keep playing? This isn't much fun today." But I always had this inner drive. I can remember when I was 15 and the decision was either I make the national team or I go back to the Canada Games program I was still eligible for. My parents wanted me to play Canada Games because it was with my own age group, but I wanted to play on the national team. They always let me make my own decisions. I was always internally motivated that way.

What made you hungry, and how have you sustained that?

I've felt since I was a young girl that I've always had something to prove in the game, primarily, I think, because I was a girl playing hockey in a male-dominated world. That's what drove me. When a lot of people would say, "Girls don't play," or "You can't play at this level," I would be like, "Just watch this. I'll prove you wrong." I think that carried me for a lot of years. As the game has been given more and more respect, I think what drives me today is that I just love to play and I want to get better. I still feel like I can become a better player. I always continue to challenge myself. It might be easy with a couple of Olympic golds to sit back and just enjoy it and say we've done well, but I still feel this fire inside. I'm already thinking, "Where am I going to train this summer to get better? Who's going to help me?" I've always tried to seek out new ways to get better and think outside the box. I've always remembered Crazy Canuck skier "Jungle" Jim Hunter's comment that it's "dumb not to be different." If you want to have success as a female playing hockey, you've got to be prepared to do what others aren't willing to do.

How did you stay hungry for the 2006 Olympics when you had already won a gold medal in 2002?

I went to Europe and played pro men's hockey in the first and second divisions with one thing in mind, to get better. It was a great experience. Prior to 2002, my husband, Thomas, a hockey coach from the Czech Republic, and I had a couple of summers of training with elite league pro teams over in Karlovy Vary in the Czech Republic. Skating with those guys and talking with people like Tom Renney and Bob Nicholson, I felt there would be an appropriate place for me to play in Europe. If I got the right situation, I felt it would be a way that I could really challenge myself. That's why I went. Every day I stepped on the ice I had to be ready to play against guys 30 or 40 pounds heavier than me. It was a very fast, physical game, even in Finland. It really helped me to improve before I returned to the women's game.

It feels like purpose and passion have played a huge part in why you're hungry.

Absolutely, I would say that those are the two key words. If you don't love the game, you can't be good at it, and I'm convinced you can't get to that top level without having a purpose, knowing what you're there to do. I think a lot of players don't know who they are. If you don't know who you are as a player and your strengths and weaknesses, it's pretty hard to make that next level or get better. That's really a key thing that you must have.

How have you helped create team hunger?

Team hunger is huge, on the women's side, especially. I find that it is the number one thing we address constantly, because we often play opponents where the outcome is already predetermined, where we dominate. I think establishing small, attainable goals helps us to keep the team hungry. For example, we want to get 50 shots on this goaltender, we want to score within the first 5 minutes of a game, we want no goals against, we want to limit the number of 2-on-1s the other team gets—all those little goals are important within the big goal of winning the game. You've got to constantly find new ways to challenge and motivate a team, whether by pushing the envelope physically or varying practices. One of the things I like a lot is doing new drills and trying new things and being creative. I think that is always exciting for a player. Playing different games, too, games within the game; you can really challenge your thinking side. Those are all things that keep you hungry.

How did you prepare for the best games you've played? What are your keys to preparation?

I would say that my biggest key is that I prepare to play the worst team the same way that I do the best team. I want to prepare every day like it's the gold-medal game so that when I get to that gold-medal game, I don't have to do any more. I just step on the ice and play. In the 2006 season we had 50 games as a team to do just that. I tried to warm up the same way and prepare mentally—what I would eat, nutrition— I would do all the things the same way. We did that as a team in the same fashion as we would have done when we hit the Olympics and, ultimately, the gold-medal game.

Give us some practical stuff for a young player maybe preparing for a game in bantam hockey.

When you eat is part of the preparation. I like to eat 3½ hours before a game, a lot of chicken and pasta and vegetables, a typical hockey player's diet. I get to the rink two hours before a game. I know exactly how I'm going to warm up. I usually go in the stands for 15 to 20 minutes with my iPod and look at the empty ice and visualize myself doing different things out there. Then, about 50 minutes before the game, I'll get my warm-up stuff on and do an off-ice warm-up, which is a lot of dynamic stretching, 10 minutes of cardio, and then some explosive agility movements to get ready for the ice. Then I get my equipment on and get ready and go out. I do that whole routine the same way every game, and after the game I cool down. The cool-down will vary. If I've played a lot of minutes that game, I do a longer cool-down than if I've played fewer minutes. Whether the game has been hard or easy also factors into how I set up my cool-down.

How did you develop your mental toughness, and what is its importance to your being the best in the world?

I think it was Larry Robinson who said the game is 85 percent mental. It *is* mental. I think part of mental toughness includes finding a way to believe in yourself at times when it seems like nobody else does. All players go through that at different levels in their career, where they're thinking, "Geez, I'm fighting for a spot on this team," and trying to make it to the next level and having a coach that maybe doesn't like them. It always comes back to that motivation from within—why you play the game—and also finding calmness in yourself, knowing that you've done everything that you can to prepare. I think if you have done that, then you're very at ease with yourself in whatever situation. Not only that, I think mental toughness is about discipline, and it's about living a lifestyle of excellence daily, not just showing up for the games. It's about how you live every day, how you sleep, how you prepare off the ice and in the off season, and not cutting corners.

Why is confidence such a hard issue to put our finger on?

Confidence is one of those things that if you have it, great, but when you lose it, it's even harder to get it back again. I think the number one issue with any player I've ever seen, male or female, is: "The coach isn't giving me confidence." I've always believed that confidence has to come from within, and when you don't have it the best thing to do, I find, is to go back to the things you do well and do them a lot. So, if you're in a practice and you just can't score, well, go back to your best move or your best shot and just work at those things. In a game, focus on those little details and break it down. When players lose confidence, they often get caught up in the big things in the game versus just simple passes, great positioning on the ice, and the little details they can pay attention to that can turn their game around. As those things happen, the confidence slowly comes back.

Let's say your confidence is waning; are there some things in your game that help bring that confidence back? I like the way you've talked about preparing for that, but are there actual trigger points for your confidence?

For example, if you're having trouble scoring, get the puck on the net. Try to have a goal of five or six shots a game. Put the puck on the net and just get quality shots, and you'd be surprised, one of those shots might just go in. If the coach isn't giving you the ice time that you want, sometimes there's nothing you can do about it. Just go out every shift and try to not work harder. I think a lot of players try to work harder, but most of the time it's about working smarter and trusting in your ability to rely on your instincts out there. I think that's a big thing. Also, in the game of hitting, when I played in men's hockey, going and getting physical often brought me right back into the game. To go out and give a hit or check somebody can really bring your confidence level up, so there are little things that really can make a difference. Let go of the outcome thoughts and "I need to score." Just completely let that go and just play the game. It's a hard thing to do, but chances are when you're able to let that go as a player, that's when confidence returns.

What helps you play at the top of your game? You've talked about preparation and confidence and mental toughness. Are there any other pieces you can tell us about that are important to playing the best game you've ever played?

It's a combination of easy speed, being sort of in that moment, and the intensity level. I find that if I'm too narrowly focused and too intense I miss passes, I miss plays, and I'm just not all there. I need a way to come in and out of that focus. You need a wide focus to play the game, but at times you also need to narrow it down, whether you're shooting on the goalie or whatever. When I have a combination of that, and when my body is physically relaxed, I'm flying out there. Those are the best games I've ever played.

I know you've had many, but pick out a few of your most exciting moments for us.

Winning the gold medal against the US in 2002 still ranks as my all-time highlight. We had a lot of adversity. We had 30 minutes of penalties in the game. It was a very intense, emotional game. That is my number one highlight.

When I was 12, I scored the winning goal at the Canada Winter Games. That was my start in the national team program and in women's hockey, so I'll always remember that goal. Playing pro in Finland and scoring my first goal over there certainly ranks up there, and probably winning the gold medal again in Torino. It was a really good tournament for our team and for me.

How important is character to being a high-performance player?

Character is everything. I always look back to the national teams I've played on and think the reason we had success was that we had great character. When you have great people it's so much less maintenance for the coaching staff. You know everyone is there for the right reasons and to do their job, and character players don't always have to be the players with a little skill, they can be your best players, as well. I do think that those intangibles in the moments where the pressure is the greatest and the stress is the highest reveal people's true character. If you have good character people on your team you always have a better chance of winning than if you have selfish people.

What are some of the setbacks that you've experienced? I'm not looking for a one, two, three, but what was the process for you to move away from adversity?

As I look back at the adversity I've faced, I would say that if I hadn't faced it I probably wouldn't have become the player that I am. Adversity is just a natural part of playing the game. Every player goes through it. You have to know as a player that there will be times of adversity; they will come and go. There are brighter spots on the horizon. The hardest thing is to stay patient with yourself and with the situation. When I was over in Europe, playing in Finland, there were times when I didn't get the ice time I would have liked, but really, it was one of the first times in my career that I was in that situation. As I played more and more games the ice time started to increase. Being away from my son was tough, but I knew that I had to do it for a bigger purpose at the time, and it all worked out in the end.

You haven't been traded, but you've played on many teams: Team Canada, Finland, and others. How did you adjust to playing for different teams?

I guess there's always a break-in period with a new team. Finland was just a totally unique situation, being the only woman playing on a men's pro team. I didn't have a conversation with one of the guys on the team until about two weeks into the season. They all spoke English, but they were shy and didn't know what to say, and I didn't know what to say. It's a very uncomfortable period, but, as a player, sometimes you have to get out of your comfort zone to get better. A new environment and change is always good. We have a lot of young rookies coming to our national team for the first time and they are absolutely horrified, excited, and nervous all at the same time. I remember what my first experience was like, as well.

Have you used the same technique to deal with personal adversity that you use in game adversity?

I think when you have adversity outside of the game of hockey, the lessons that you learn from playing the game can really help you a lot in your personal life, particularly the whole idea of being patient and letting things come and letting things go. I just think of myself as a player. I think that five years ago, when things would happen in a game or a coach would do something or we'd lose a game or were on a losing streak, I would just dwell on it for way too long. Now I feel like I'm much more patient as a player and as a person, and I'm able to let those things go. This really helps you perform better because you're not carrying all that baggage. If you have baggage off the ice, you probably have baggage on the ice. It's an important part of being a hockey player to be able to leave the things that are bothering you off the ice behind when you get on the ice. When I was a young girl growing up and playing hockey, the ice was sort of my safe haven. I hated having to change in a separate dressing room or out in the lobby or in the bathroom, but when I got on the ice I knew that most of the parents wouldn't know which one was the girl out there and I would just be able to play. And, there's always something to look forward to no matter how bad the situation is.

When have you felt the most pressure and how did you handle it? Were you successful in your mind?

I felt the most pressure when I was playing for a gold medal at the Olympics or a World Championship final. The great thing about being on a hockey team in those final games is that you have 20 other players who can share in that pressure. It's a very important point to remember that it's never just about one player. I find I can deflect that pressure just by focusing on my job, what I can do out there, what people expect me to do, and that's all I can do. There are so many things that are out of your control as a player. You have to understand that to handle pressure, and accept that you can't control it as much as you'd like. Pressure comes and goes, but pressure can't always be there. I think it can really tire you out as a player and as a person if you are always feeling like you are under pressure. Most of the time players put pressure on themselves. Focusing on what you do well as a player and on what you can control within the game takes the pressure away.

What were the qualities of the closest-knit team that you've played on?

Trust, a real honest trust in the room, where you know the next person's got your back and is there to support you. I've been on teams where not everybody liked each other, but we still had great chemistry as a team because we were there for a common purpose and we left our disagreements outside the door. For a close-knit team, I think you have to have a great combination of youth and experience, of outgoing and more reserved players, and a coaching staff that understands that.

How do teams build, sustain, and maintain trust?

I am not one for real team building, it's not really my style, and I've done a lot with the national team over the years. I've found that the best team building we've done is when we've done actual events. We did a triathlon with the National Women's Team in Prince Edward Island in an actual team format. You'd be amazed to see how others react to helping when people are truly scared or truly under stress, and how much that can build the on-ice situation with your team. We have also climbed mountains, with some players who were absolutely horrified of heights, and the team had to work through that. I find that those real events you can do with a team, versus sitting in a room and writing something on a piece of paper, go a longer way toward building that chemistry and that trust.

Can a team still function at a high level when there are players who don't get along?

Absolutely. I've been a part of many teams where players don't get along and don't like each other. You don't have to like each other, but the common thing you have to have is respect. If you respect the other person's contribution to the team, you can definitely be successful.

Describe a great team player.

I think a great team player is somebody who knows their role, their contribution to the team, and does that very well. At the end of the day this player cares more about the team winning than any sort of personal goals or accomplishments. It is somebody who is willing to give of themselves, of their energy and time, rather than just show up and leave. A great team player gets involved and cares and shows that in many different ways.

Have you ever had to put aside personal values to fit in as part of a team?

Certainly there have been coaches whose style I didn't like or agree with. There have been different events or activities that our team has done over the years that I wouldn't have chosen to do myself, but you do them because it's the right thing for the team to do. There are times when you do have to do that, but I don't think you, as a player, should ever compromise your core values or beliefs for a team. Sometimes you have to stand up for what's right. I'm speaking maybe to the hazing or some of those things that you see in hockey. It doesn't happen that often, but sometimes as a player you have to trust your gut and say, "Hey, this conduct or behaviour is not right, and I should stand up."

You mentioned the influence of your dad when you were a young player, but did you have an idol in the game of hockey?

I loved the Oilers of the 1980s, so I had Gretzky and Messier to look up to. As I get older I admire more and more players in the game and a lot of people I've met. Bob Clarke has been a good friend of mine for a number of years, and he's helped me just by chatting about different things in the game. I have a lot of respect for how good the best players in the game are now, and I love to watch what they do and to learn from them.

Who influenced your development to become the best in the world?

My parents, when I was very young, but later Wally Kozak, Shannon Miller, Mel Davidson, just Hockey Canada in general and the national team program all helped me to develop. I've grown up through the national team program, really, as a player, so I think they've helped me a lot.

For some of our younger readers, throughout all of this high-performance hockey, right from 12 up, how did you handle the balance of school and the commitment to the game?

It was very clear to me when I was in grade 10 and playing on the national team that there were only two things in my life at the time: school and hockey. I think if you really want to be great at the game and at school you have to be aware of that. You must have good time-management skills, be organized and be able to set aside time to do your work, because there is more to life than hockey, and an education is definitely an important part of it. Not everybody is going to make a million bucks playing the game.

Living or dead, who do you admire most and why?

I would say my parents, for everything that they've been able to do for me, and my younger brother and sister. My parents are both schoolteachers. If I were a male player playing in the NHL, I would be able to finance their retirment by now. They are still working and travelling to the Olympic Games and doing all those things. They really instilled in me a love for being active and for following my dreams. They never pressured us into playing as kids. They just let us make our own decisions and that's something I'm grateful for.

If you could choose one person to be your neighbour, who pops to your mind and why?

This is definitely coming from a female. I would say Oprah. I've always admired her for the influence that she has on people of the world and the great success she's had with her career and how she makes an impact on the world and the people's lives that she has touched. She seems like a very interesting person, and I've always enjoyed watching her show, so she might be neat to have coffee with.

If you had another job outside of the game, what would it be?

I love medicine. I have a passion for it. I think if I was not involved in the game I would probably go to med school. I'd love to spend a year in Africa working in some of the refugee camps or with the UN, fighting AIDS. Those are things I was always interested in as a kid, and when I'm finished playing, probably things I will pursue.

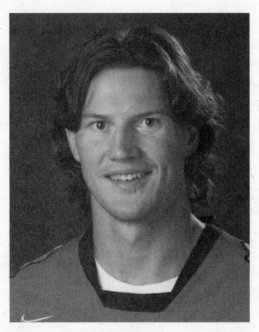

Shane Doan

Born in Halkirk, Alberta, Shane Doan is a modern-NHL anomaly, having played his entire 11-seasons-plus career with the same franchise. Drafted seventh overall in 1995 by the Winnipeg Jets, he moved with that team to Phoenix and is the only current Coyote to have once donned a Jets' jersey.

Doan played major junior with the Kamloops Blazers for three seasons, winning back-to-back Memorial Cup championships in 1994 and 1995, when he was selected to the Memorial Cup All-Star Team and awarded the Stafford Smythe Trophy as the tournament's Most Valuable Player. Not surprisingly, Shane was among the first group of players to be honoured as Blazer Legends 10 years later, in 2005.

Shane made his mark in professional hockey immediately, being named the Winnipeg Jets Rookie of the Year in 1996. He scored at least 20 goals in seven consecutive seasons from 1999 to 2007. The consummate all-round hockey player, Doan was the only NHL player to register over 200 hits and over 200 shots on goal in 2001–02. He was proclaimed the Coyotes' Hardest Working Player in 1999–00, 2001–02, and 2002–03.

In the 2003–04 season, Doan became the Coyotes' captain, played in the NHL All-Star Game, led the Coyotes with 68 points and captured the Coyotes' Most Valuable Player and Three Star awards.

Even better-known north of the 49th parallel for his inspired international play, Doan helped Team Canada finish fourth at the 1999 World Hockey Championships and win a gold medal at the 2003 World Hockey Championships. In 2004 he scored the tie-breaking and game-winning goal for Canada in the World Cup of Hockey final. Doan was unable to play at the 2004 World Championships because of injury, but as an alternate captain he helped lead Team Canada to a silver finish at the 2005 World Championships. He played for Team Canada in the 2006 Olympics and was captain of Canada's 2007 undefeated gold-medal-winning World Championship team, scoring a hat trick in a span of 6 minutes and 25 seconds while political controversy over his choice as captain brewed at home.

Shane comes from a decidedly athletic family: his father, Bernie, was drafted in 1971 by the St. Louis Blues, his sister Leighann plays professional basketball in France, and his cousin Bart is a rodeo cowboy and Calgary Olympic Oval icemaker who is married to gold-medal-winning speed skater Catriona Le May Doan. Shane and wife Andrea have four children, who may yet decide to take up the torch.

The Interview

In your mind, what kind of leadership works in NHL dressing rooms?

You have to lead by example. So many coaches tell you what's right and how to do it, then you have an opportunity to read books and talk to different players, and you have your own opportunities and experiences. In the end I believe that it is easy to talk the talk, but much harder to walk the walk. Teppo Numminen was a phenomenal leader. The guys that I respected and admired the most were the ones who didn't talk much, but just did what they knew was right and did it the best that they could. They set an example.

You've been a leader for a long time now; what is the essence of leadership?

It sounds almost kind of corny, but I think it's really putting the group ahead of your personal agenda. As a leader there are times when you might want something that would be beneficial to you and yet you know that it's probably not what's best for the group. Someone who is willing to constantly put the group ahead of himself is showing leadership. Leadership is also being able to stand up when the time is right and make the unpopular decision and say, "Hey, you may not want to hear this, but this is what it is: we're not fooling ourselves pretending that this is right and the way we're going is right." Sometimes you have to do that.

Who are the best leaders that you've played with and what were the qualities that made them that way?

Teppo Numminen was one of the better leaders that I've played with, and he didn't say boo. He didn't say anything, but worked harder than anybody else on the ice. He never ever cut a corner; he always did it the way it was supposed to be done. His discipline gave him authority; I think discipline is so important.

Keith Tkachuk was a leader in a different way. His authority and presence came from his passion and intensity. I played with Joe Sakic and Mario Lemieux at the World Cup. They were respected players. Obviously, their skill earned them the respect of their teammates, but it was much more than that. Your leaders have to be guys that are respected.

You've worn a "C" for a long time. What are your leadership qualities?

The important thing for me is to let the guys know that I would do anything that I would expect them to do. I've been able to play on the fourth line, the third line, the second line, and the first line, so I've been able to understand the dynamics of each. If you're a guy who has to stay out and work hard after practice and do the skates, then that's what you have to do; I've been there and done that. If you're the guy who plays 25 minutes a night, I've been able to do that.

So that's one of my strengths. I understand everyone's role. I appreciate so much that it's hard to be a guy who plays eight minutes a night and is expected to contribute in those eight minutes. If the team doesn't win, you might be one of the guys who sit out. It's not going to be the first-line guy, even though, realistically, in your eight minutes, what can you do?

Dealing with that is one of the hardest things in hockey, and I was that guy for four years, sitting on the bench and not really getting anywhere. I found that a lot harder than now, playing 25 minutes a night, knowing that if I've had a bad shift I'm going to get to go back out. I think that's one of the strengths of my leadership, that I appreciate and respect what guys have to go through in every single position.

How important are the "glue guys," who don't necessarily wear an "A" or a "C," to the team and in the room?

They are the essence of what makes a team successful, these guys who can back up your leader. If you have one guy saying it, it doesn't really accomplish anything, but if you can have two or three guys saying it, then you bring in a few more guys, and all of a sudden it becomes the mentality of your whole team. You can have the best leader in the world, but if he doesn't have the right group of guys following him, you're not going to have any success. He needs a core group who are his guys, who he can rely on. The players who are willing to do whatever it takes to win are the glue guys who hold everyone together. You are never going to have everyone on the same page all the time. That pressure to get everyone on the same page has to come from within the group. If just one player is doing it by himself, that's not enough, it's useless, but if you have a group of guys, that makes the difference. Even if they disagree with what the leader is saying, to be able to stand behind him and back it up is key.

What do you respect about some of the coaches that you've played for?

The one I respect the most is Bobby Francis, who once won the NHL Coach of the Year Award. As a player I would do anything for him, because he cared more about me as a person than as a player. He wanted to win. He would push my buttons and get me fired up and be mad at me and in my face, even embarrassing me by calling me out in the media or in the dressing room, but I knew when it was all said and done that he was doing it to get the most out of me, because I knew he cared more about me as a person than as a player. He could whip me and beat me all he wanted, but I knew that at the end of the day he was doing it for a reason.

Is that the way that coaches get the best out of you, by showing they care?

For me personally, yes. To a certain degree I need to know that he cares about me, but it's also important to know that there's an agenda. If you want to call me out and embarrass me to make me better in certain situations, by all means do it. If you're doing it just to play mind games,

I don't want anything to do with that. I'm in a different situation now, having been in the league for several years. It changes the way you view coaches, but it's important for me to know that I will do what you ask when I know that you respect me.

How much of motivating players is the coach's job, and how much comes from the players?

I believe a large amount comes from the coach. You have to be an emotional player, to a certain degree, in order for the coach to really have a motivational effect on you. If the coach can recognize that you're an emotional guy, then he knows triggering your emotions can tend to fire you up and get you going for the first part of the game. That doesn't carry for the whole game or for the whole year, but every now and then, I think it is important for a coach to go to that emotional level, whether it's getting a guy mad, pumping his tires, challenging him to his face or challenging him in the media. On the other hand, some guys just aren't emotional and you're not going to be able to motivate them; it has to come from them.

How do you like a coach to communicate? Is it better to be pushed or patted on the back?

I think I'm right in between. Bobby Francis came after me hard one time and embarrassed me. I think we were playing Minnesota. He just called me out in front of the guys. I was obviously upset, but I never said anything back. He knew that he was hitting a nerve, and he left me alone for the next three games, which was unusual because usually Bobby would come and talk to me after the game, after we had calmed down. When he finally came to talk to me, his theory was that I had played really well the last three games, but it took him embarrassing me in front of my teammates and me approaching it with the "I'll prove you wrong" attitude [to get me to play that way]. He then said, "Now that I've come to you, if you let that go back down again I will do it so much worse." If he hadn't let me know that I was playing better but that if I let it drop he'd be in my face I don't think it would have had such a long-term impact. I think I needed to be knocked upside the head a little bit sometimes, but at the same time his coming to me after and explaining the reason really helped. In fact I went on a run of a month and a half or two months where I was scoring and doing everything well, and it kind of kept me going for the rest of the year. He just left me alone. So I think it's a little bit of both for me.

What do you like about Wayne Gretzky as a coach?

Wayne's knowledge of the game. He's played so many games—I didn't realize how many games it was—and every game you play in the league, you learn something new. The fact that he played for so many seasons really gave Wayne a vast knowledge of the game. I think another of Wayne's strengths is that he encourages players to use their hockey sense; he tries not to harness guys too much. Wayne encourages us to use our hockey sense and be players. I think whenever a coach is like that, he is going to get the most out of his team. It comes down to having the freedom to be creative, and Wayne encourages creativity.

You've been on a lot of winning teams. What is the difference between a winning environment and a losing environment?

On every successful team, the roles for each individual are clearly defined. When we were in Toronto with the World Cup team, everyone knew that Mario was our number-one line. Whatever line he was on was the number-one line. I think it took a lot of the pressure off the number-two, number-three and number-four line, which I was on. We knew our job was to be hard to play against and match up against the other team's top line: just be pests and just do whatever we could to make the night as long as we possibly could for the other team's top line. So, it gave the freedom for guys to kind of be more themselves inside their roles. Obviously, I play a different role with the Coyotes, but I think it gave me more freedom to just be myself in that role. It always seems to be that way in international tournaments. When you bring guys together, the more clearly the roles are defined by the coaching staff and the management, the more the guys tend to excel in each of their roles.

I think that's so important. You can't have a fourth-line guy that feels like his eight minutes of ice time aren't worth anything, because that's unacceptable. In his eight minutes, his goal is to be physical and to provide energy. When I get out there, the coaching staff are not expecting me to beat the whole team and score and make an amazing play, they're expecting me to win that battle along the blue line, they're expecting me to get the puck deep, and they're expecting me to get a forecheck going. If that's all I do, that's successful. Knowing your role and playing it well breeds a positive atmosphere, and a positive atmosphere is the most important thing in winning.

You've talked about what coaches and managers can do. What can players do to really influence a winning environment?

Players need to embrace their roles and be willing to accept a role different than what they might have had at the beginning of the year, to be the best that they can be at checking or at being a power-play guy or a penalty-kill guy. I played with Mike Sullivan, who loved to kill penalties. I mean, he killed them as well as anybody. You could actually feel a boost on the bench when he did his job. When he's out there blocking shots, always in the right spot, there's a boost on the bench of: "You know what? I've got to do my job better." If Sully's role was to be a goal scorer, then it might have been a different situation for him. It really comes down to fulfilling your own individual role. If that happens, I think the group gets better.

It's so important to be together as a group to be successful and also to be willing to hear somebody say something bad about you. That's tough coming from a teammate, and I think that you can only accept it if that teammate is willing to be with you, to be friends. It's hard for me to accept from a guy that I don't really know well, who just comes in and automatically tells me what he thinks.

What motivates or drives you? Did you always have it as a youngster?

I think I've pretty much always had that drive to a certain degree. Anybody that makes it to the NHL has it. Well, maybe not. There are a lot of guys who are a lot more skilled than me that might not need it as much, but since I'm not as skilled as those guys, I need to have a lot more drive. I need that willingness to outwork a guy and that willingness to outgrunt a guy, and to take pride in that. I think that drive's always been there with me. My dad told me that it's something that I was to hold on to and make sure that I could control. Because I couldn't control that other stuff, it drove me. If I didn't succeed, then it was my fault because I could control how hard I worked.

How do you, as a captain, create that team hunger?

I think you can always be better. That's true for everyone in sports. There is never such a thing as playing the perfect game in any sport, but you still want to achieve that perfect game. You could maybe shoot the puck harder or hit an opponent harder or be in the right spot more often. There's always more for me to learn, and as a team, it comes down to proving yourself over and over again. There's nothing better than knowing you're the best—and if you win, then you're the best. There's pride that comes with a certain degree of knowing that you're the best, and there's a huge amount of desire that comes with knowing that I need to win. I don't know exactly how to put my finger on it: losing is just no fun, and I really want to win.

So the hunger drives you toward the win and toward being better?

For sure, because as an athlete I've become so goal-oriented in what I do. You're focused on achieving whatever the goal is in front of you. So the hungrier you are, the more willing you are to push through stuff that makes you uncomfortable. That's definitely always been there for me. I remember in minor hockey when you're losing a game, or you're on the ice and you can't score, and there are tears streaming down your face as you're trying to skate. You're thinking, "It's just a game, just relax," but there are tears running down your face. The tears come because you want to win so badly.

How do you prepare best for games?

It really depends. It can vary from time to time according to the way that I'm playing. You can almost overhype yourself. I can sometimes get too hyped up for a game, and it takes a half a period to settle in and play the way I'm supposed to. Other times I can be too down and have to get myself up. I have to be pretty balanced. The more I focus on being physical and keeping my feet moving, then the rest of my game will take care of itself. The simpler I can prepare, the better I'll be. If I'm thinking about the game too much, like, "What's our forecheck? What's our neutral zone system?" I get away from focusing on "Let's just simplify what I need to do." I know what our system is, so I have to just make sure my feet are moving and I'm physical. Sometimes I start to struggle trying to think about too many things: I need to be in this position, I've got to be here, I've got to be there. That's so counterproductive for me.

How did you develop your mental toughness?

I don't know if I ever have. I think it's something every single player struggles with. I really do believe that everyone thinks that they can be just a little bit tougher, just a little bit more mentally focused, but I think my mental toughness came more from experience than anything. You might go a bunch of games without scoring, but that doesn't mean that you should change the way you play. Mentally you just kind of grind it out. Sometimes when it feels like you're not ever going to score again, you start to get down on yourself and start to pressure yourself. Mental toughness and the ability to work through it comes with a bit of experience. Talking to other players has helped me out, because there are times when I wonder if I'm ever going to mentally be able to grind it out and do what I need to do. You see it so often when guys get called up to play one game. They'll be unbelievable, and then mentally they just can't hold it. They need that toughness to be able to say, "That's the player I am. This player who's struggling right now, that's not who I am." When you grasp that, I think it makes the game easier.

Why is confidence so hard to put our finger on?

I wish I knew! If you ask any player, they'll agree with this: "If I score a goal in the first period, I am going to be twice the player; you are going to have your hands full trying to stop me for the rest of the game." It's so important in the NHL to have a tandem of two guys going on a team, because there are going to be nights when a guy doesn't have it, and all of a sudden he gets an empty net and he gets his confidence. If a centre makes a great play and gives you an empty net and you score, but you really didn't do anything other than put the puck in the net, you still get a boost of confidence.

It comes back to what we were talking about earlier; it's the confidence to believe that you are that good player and not the player that's struggling. I guess that's mental toughness too. I think those go hand in hand. Confidence is about really believing that I'm the guy who can score, the guy who can go out and dominate a game, the guy who can go out and have a game where everything works. That's who I am. The player who just turned the puck over or made that mistake is not me. That's not who I really am.

It's hard to continually have that level of confidence, but if you could ever master it, you would be a more consistent and durable player. You often hear players say when they aren't scoring, "I can't score." Very rarely do you hear guys say, "I can score; I can score." I think that the guys who are good truly believe that they can score. They just believe that. They have such confidence that they don't care if you stop them a hundred times, they still believe they are good enough to score. There are other guys who are more talented, but they aren't so sure they can score. They could score on you 10 times, but if they miss three or four in a row they literally believe that they can't score. I believe the difference is training your mind, and that comes back to mental toughness, where you say to yourself, "I'm the guy who can score, not the guy who can't."

Tell us about one of your most exciting moments in hockey.

The game-winning goal I scored in the World Cup against Finland was absolutely unbelievable. When Joe Thornton passed it to me behind the net and I caught the puck, I knew that the guy had fallen. Lehtinen and I were battling in the corner. Then I was walking to the net and Kiprusoff went down early. I knew I had him beaten, and it seemed like forever, but I knew I had scored. I knew he'd gone down and I knew there was no help coming, and that I had all the time in the world to walk across the net and score. It was one of the weirdest things, and one of the best feelings I've ever had. It was just awesome. I literally remember thinking, "I just scored in the final game." It was a lot of fun, and that was even before the puck was in the net. I knew it was going to happen, and it seemed to take forever for it go in. That was kind of unique for me.

How important is character to being a high-performance player?

If you're going to have any kind of duration in your career, you have to have character. There's going to be adversity somewhere along the line, and character is what is really going to dictate how you come out of it. I believe character is so important. You need the player who can score 80 or 90 points to make the playoffs, but you need that one character guy to win game seven in the playoffs. When it's on the line, it's the character guy that comes up with the goal in game seven. When all the chips are down and you need to win that game, you need that character guy on your team. He might not get the opportunity to do that if you don't have the 90- or 100-point player doing his thing, but when it comes right down to it, it's always the character guy that steps up and comes up big.

Describe for us a time when you were in a slump, not producing. How do you get out of a difficult time?

I remember one year I went 35 or 37 games in a row without scoring to start the season. I had a 0 in the stat column for at least 37 games in a row and it was so hard. This was my third or fourth year in the league, and I remember thinking, "I'm never ever going to get over this. I don't know what to do. I didn't think I was that bad; apparently I am." I remember thinking along that line, and then once I scored, I scored seven or eight in the next 25 games. It wasn't until I realized those things weren't true, that I wasn't that bad a player, that I was able to get through it by thinking, "You know what? I am good and I do believe that I can score and I will score." Sometimes you've got to realize it's just not going to go in the net and you need to contribute in other ways.

How do you adjust to a new team? Is it usually a time of adversity for players or do they handle it pretty well?

I've been with the Coyotes so long that I have seen guys come in and handle it well and others not so well. There's a real fine line between coming in and asserting yourself in the dressing room and inserting yourself into the team. As a teammate and as a player, your job is to encourage your teammates. It is your coach's job to point out mistakes. So coming into a new team, it's important to encourage and pump up everyone's tires. It is also important to kind of find your place: "What's my role going to be with this team? Am I going to be the guy who lightens up the room, or the guy who talks lots, or the guy who should be quiet in the corner and do my job as well as I can?" I think with every team it varies, but it comes down to making sure that everybody on the team knows that when all is said and done, the thing I care about most is how we do as a group, more than how I do as an individual.

How has personal adversity affected the way you play the game?

Whenever personal adversity comes, it almost seems like it's a release to play the game. When I'm playing, when I'm on the ice, I don't remember ever thinking about anything but my job and what I've got to do. So you almost look forward to playing the game. This last year I went through it over at the World Championships in Russia. It was actually really nice to be playing. I really enjoyed the games. I didn't have to worry. I wasn't thinking about anything else when I was playing.

Just walk us through what happened over in Moscow. ("L'affaire Doan" erupted shortly after Shane Doan was chosen to captain Team Canada at the 2007 World Championships. Bloc Québécois leader Gilles Duceppe called this "an insult to Quebecers." Hockey Canada officials were subsequently summoned to Parliament, where they defended their choice by reminding the Canadian government that the NHL had cleared Doan of all charges after investigating the December 13, 2005, Coyotes/Canadiens game in which Doan was accused of having uttered an anti-French remark to a francophone linesman.)

I take a huge amount of pride in the fact that I get to play for my country. A Team Canada jersey was the first jersey I ever owned, and whenever they ask me to play for Canada I will always say yes. There might come a day when they don't want me to play, but until that day comes I'm going to keep saying yes.

When they asked me to give up my captaincy, it bothered me quite a bit when I wasn't at the arena. I was thinking about it and hearing about it, and people were talking about it and asking me, "Do you think you should give it up?" and "What are you going to do about it?" I was thinking, "I guess it comes down to if that's what's best for the group, then that's what I'm going to do." Yet when I was at the rink, it was almost like, "Well, I came to the rink and no one told me to give it up. I'm going to do the best job I can today." When we were at the rink, none of that really came into the dressing room. Obviously, that was a huge blessing, because the coaching staff and the players and my teammates were so supportive. It was almost a relief. It was a break from everything that was going on outside. It really emphasized how much I enjoy the game. I just love to play, and when I didn't have to think about the adversity that I was having personally, it was kind of a break from it all. When I was out playing, it wasn't on my mind. You're prepared and mentally ready to go, you're not thinking, "I wonder what they think. Should I really be doing this?" Once you're committed to it, you do it.

What are the qualities of a closely knit team?

I think you need to have the guy who keeps the room light. That's so important. It seems that on every team that wins, there are always one or two guys that you love. There's the guy that everyone laughs at. He's the guy who always cracks a joke here and there, who does something stupid or does something funny, and it's done in an appropriate way. It's funny, but not embarrassing to anybody. That's important to have in the room, because you're playing a sport where you have to have fun. If you don't have fun, you don't have creativity. Creativity comes directly from having fun. You see that the guys who are really creative tend to just love the game. Guys that aren't as creative feel like it's a job they have to work at.

With regard to chemistry, it's important if you're going to have fun as a team that you also have one or two guys who will stand up when the coaches aren't in the room and challenge the team. They might say, "Hey, this isn't right. We need to be better as a group. You and I know it. Let's get our act together." The guys have to respect whoever those players are. This can't be coming from somebody they don't respect. If you can have the right group of guys filling the right roles, finding their spots, then chemistry tends to happen on its own.

Does winning breed chemistry, or does chemistry breed winning?

The more you win, the easier it is to have fun, and I really believe that having fun is one of the most important things. I know that you can go into a room that's dead and in the end you're not going to win. I don't know why, but you just can't compare it to a team that's full of life and laughing and enjoying it. It's got to be appropriate. I'm not saying that it's not a serious thing. But at the same time, if you're not having fun playing, then you're not creative, and if you're not creative, you're not going to win.

How important is trust on a team?

Being together for an amount of time has made Detroit so successful. They've built up trust. If someone points out your mistakes and you trust the fact that he cares and respects you as a person, then you can listen to him. If you don't trust him, and you think he's doing it to be malicious or vindictive, his advice is going to be useless. So yes, trust is huge. When you can trust the other person's opinions and trust that your teammates are going to do their job, then you can focus more on doing yours.

Can you describe a great team player?

A great team player is one of your leaders. He is the one that consciously puts the group before his own personal good. If that means being willing to play a more defensive role, or block shots, or not cheat offensively, or stay on the defensive side of the puck, or take that hit along the boards, then that's what he has to do. As I said earlier, the team players are the character guys that you must have to win game seven.

As a younger player, did you have an idol?

When I was a kid I played defence, so Paul Coffey was the player I wanted to emulate. He could skate, and did everything, offensively. Then I realized that I was always trying to be up the ice anyway, so I switched to playing forward when I got to junior. I then wanted to be like any player who was a little bit physical and was a bigger forward, like Cam Neely. He and Clark Gillies were the guys who created the power forward role. Gordie Howe was the original power forward, but I was able to watch Cam Neely and see what he did and how he battled so hard, so he was one of those players I really looked up to and wanted to pattern my game after. Obviously, no one has ever matched him since. He was pretty incredible.

What kind of effect did your parents have on your minor hockey journey?

I truly believe that my dad is still the best coach in the world. If he decided to coach right now, his team would be successful, because he understands the game and he also understands how to encourage people and be very, very firm. My dad was a huge influence on the way that I played, instilling in me the desire to work hard and have fun. My mom and dad both instilled that, but from my mom's side it was also, "You'd better hate to lose." My mom hated to lose even more than my dad.

Who, living or dead, do you admire most and why?

Is it okay if I go with the Biblical thing?

Actually, Scott Niedermayer picked Jesus.

No kidding! I would have to go with Peter, one of the Apostles. I would love to be able to talk to him, because he made mistakes, huge mistakes, and yet still managed to accept them. I understand that Jesus forgave him, but it's one thing to understand that you've been forgiven and another thing to live with that. He was able to live with that and be such an incredible man, and yet at the same time he had made such an obvious mistake and is noted for it. It would be great to sit and have a conversation with him about that. I don't know if I want anyone to talk about my mistakes, but if he would be willing to talk to me about the way that he handled it, the way he lived his life after, that would be special. He's the guy that I've always admired.

Jarome Iginla

Born on Canada Day in 1977 in Edmonton, Alberta, Jarome Iginla is every Canadian minor hockey player's dream on and off the ice. Jarome entered the Western Hockey League as a Kamloops Blazer at the tender age of 16 and proceeded to stack up personal and team awards. En route to winning the first of two Memorial Cups with the Blazers, Jarome was awarded the George Parsons Trophy as the Memorial Cup's most sportsmanlike player in 1995. He was selected to the WHL's West First All-Star Team in 1996, was named the WHL's Most Valuable Player in 1996 and also to the Canadian Hockey League's First All-Star Team in his final junior season.

The Dallas Stars selected Jarome Iginla as their first-round pick in 1995 when the draft was held in his hometown of Edmonton, and then, while he was still a junior hockey player, traded him to the Calgary Flames in December.

Iginla scored a goal and an assist in two playoff games when called up to the Flames in the spring of 1996 before joining them full time the following season for a spectacular NHL debut that culminated in Iginla's

selection to the All-Rookie Team and finish as runner-up to the Rookie
of the Year.

In 2002 Jarome Iginla became the first player of African descent to
win the regular season NHL goal- and point-scoring titles with a total of
52 goals and 96 points. He was also selected by his peers to win the Lester
B. Pearson Award as the NHL's best player and was a nominee for both the
Hart and King Clancy Memorial trophies.

Iginla was named the Flames captain in 2003, and his 41 goals that
season were enough to win him a three-way tie for the goal-scoring title. .
He played in three consecutive NHL All-Star Games in 2002, 2003, and
2004 and won both the King Clancy Memorial Trophy for humanitarian
contributions and the NHL Foundation Award for Community Service
in 2004. On December 7, 2006, Jarome scored his 300th career goal and
600th career point, and capped off the month by becoming the Molson
Cup Award Winner and the NHL's First Star for the month of December.
On February 24, 2007, Jarome scored his 100th career power-play goal
and passed Joe Nieuwendyk, the player he had been traded for back in
1995, for second spot on the all-time Flames goal scorers list.

Jarome Iginla is an equally accomplished international player. He
represented Canada in the 1996 World Junior Championships, bringing
home a gold medal from Boston along with a First Team All-Star
selection, top scorer (12 points in 6 games) and outstanding forward
awards. He also won gold medals for Team Canada in 1997 at the World
Championships and the 2004 World Cup of Hockey, and he helped
Canada capture its first Olympic gold medal in 50 years at the 2002
Winter Olympics before competing a second time for Canada at the
2006 Olympics. Jarome Iginla is indeed a champion on and off the ice
who has made all Canadians proud.

The Interview

Were you selected in the Western Hockey League bantam draft?

No, I wasn't originally drafted in the bantam draft. Then for some reason, maybe because of the number of players available, they decided to have a roll-over draft a couple of weeks later, and at that time I was drafted by Kamloops. Originally, I was very disappointed not to be drafted. I was at school and playing hockey, and all of my teammates were all eager about the draft. I had received a lot of letters of interest from quite a few teams, probably in the teens. One team that talked to me thought I could play at 16. I had other teammates that had one letter or no letters, and they got drafted, so to be honest, it was a big disappointment. I was surprised because I was scoring and having a good year compared to other rookies in the league. For me, it was the first really huge disappointment.

How did that affect you as a bantam player?

It was hard, but it was a good learning experience. Just thinking about it and talking with my grandpa made me more determined. It was also humbling, at the time. I was one of the higher-scoring rookies in the league, and as a result I had almost expected to be drafted. I was hoping and just waiting for a call. It was a good eye-opener, and I tried to use it in a positive way, but it took a few days to see it that way.

And from there what was your first training camp in Kamloops like?

My first camp was held in the Sherwood Park area in the spring, so it was close to where I lived in St. Albert. There wasn't that much pressure because it was just all the prospects, not the players that were actually on the team. I didn't go to the main camp at 15 because of baseball. I was

16 at the first real camp that I can remember going to. It was pretty cool. I had watched the Blazers, they were on Channel 10 at home, and I was able to watch and learn a bit about the team before I went there.

I remember my mom driving me to Kamloops and then dropping me off with the family and stuff. That was pretty tough. I wasn't crying or anything, but at the same time it was scary going to a new school and it was a different style of hockey. In minor hockey everything is fun and everybody gets to play, and then all of a sudden I go to camp and there's fighting. It was a big adjustment.

Who are the best leaders you've ever played with, and what were their qualities?

Joe Sakic and Steve Yzerman come to mind right away. They were the best leaders that I ever played with at the NHL level. I always thought guys were born with pure talent and were so successful because they were so skilled, but then I got a chance to play with Sakic and Yzerman at the 2002 Olympics and saw what great shape they were in and how hard they worked on and off the ice. Also, seeing a guy like Al McInnis was an eye-opener. I realized that they worked really hard in all areas of their game. Their preparation before the game, their routines, and all that stuff, it was impressive.

I'll just tell you a quick story from the 2002 Olympics. Every day I was excited to see whose line I would be on. I was one of the younger players, so I didn't know if guys would be excited to be on my line or not. The first day I was very excited to play with Steve Yzerman and Brendan Shanahan, but it didn't go well for our team. There was a shift in lines, and Joe Sakic went from playing with Mario Lemieux and Paul Kariya to playing with me and Simon Gagne. I was thinking, "He's probably not too happy about this." I'm not sure how he felt, but I remember him coming up to us right away and saying, "I'm excited to be playing with you guys. Let's have some fun," in such a subtle way it made me feel more comfortable. It definitely relieved all the pressure. Those subtle things made a huge difference in making me comfortable on that line. Mario Lemieux was also very approachable in the tournament. They were such big stars, but they treated everybody around them with a lot of respect, and they are humble guys.

What do you feel your strongest leadership qualities to be?

I like to compete. I love the competition. I don't know if that's a leadership quality or not. I really just enjoy the battles and the passion. I just love playing hockey and love competing. Hopefully it helps the team. I also enjoy playing with guys when I see their love of the game.

Are you vocal in the room?

I don't talk a lot. I mean, I talk a lot in a normal setting. Guys will probably tell you I talk too much. I love to debate and argue and things like that, but in the dressing room I'm not one of the most vocal guys. Over the years I probably grew more and more comfortable saying different things, but not a ton. I definitely am not one of the most vocal in the room.

Are you put in a position to confront players or is that not something that you like to do?

On the ice and just as a teammate, not because I'm captain, I like talking to players about how we can improve. The guys may have suggestions for me, but just as my teammates. Darryl Sutter was a demanding coach, and he let us know when we weren't going, so I think on our team, as a teammate, I'd rather encourage, and it feels better to be encouraged. I know when I'm playing bad, and we all know when the puck feels square. And for that day, when I just feel I can't do anything right, it doesn't feel good when a teammate comes and yells at me and tells me what I already know. From my point of view I'm probably more on the side of trying to be a bit more positive and not really big-time confrontational, which at times some people do very well, but that's not really my style.

How important is leadership from inside the room, from a dressing-room-out point of view?

I think it's very important. There are a lot of different personalities, so I think it's important that everybody respects one another. Not everyone's going to play the same way. Some guys are more physical, some come across more heated, so it's important to respect one another and have the same goals and be professionals. Leadership on the team is not up to one or two players, or the captains and assistant captains. I really think it's everybody feeling they are a part of it and having a different role. Whether some guys are more vocal, and some guys are more energy guys, everybody has a role and they can take pride in being an equal part of the leadership, not just on the ice.

What do you respect most about the coaches you have played for?

I think communication is the biggest thing. It never feels good when you're not going. I think it's better to be told. Sometimes you play and you feel like you're going alright, then you realize the coach isn't happy at all, and then all of a sudden you're sitting out and you have no idea why. I know with Darryl, and it was the same in junior with Don Hay, you know where you stand. You know what's expected of you, in fairness to you. When you're going well it's nice to hear that the coaches are happy, that they like what you're doing, and not necessarily in front of everybody. When you're not going, sometimes I guess it comes across as harder because sometimes coaches do it in a lousy way, but I think it's important for them to let every player know where they stand. I think it's important for the coaching staff to let every player know consistently what they're happy with and where the players need to improve. With some coaches, a guy will just be sitting out and have no clue why, even though he felt he was just starting to go. I guess communication is number one.

How do coaches get the best out of Jarome Iginla?

Confidence is a big part of the game for players. I've been in the league nine years, and I think it's just as important today as it was my first or second year. The more confidence the coach shows in me, the more confidence I have. I guess it shouldn't always be the case, but that's probably the biggest thing.

What gives you confidence from a coaching point of view?

I think consistency and communication. It helps when the coaches let me know if they want something different from me, as far as my play or style of play. I'm a power forward and I'm always trying to find that balance between the physical side and the finesse side, and sometimes I'm maybe not as physical as I should be or vice versa. I think the coach's communication can help me along those lines. Consistency is also important because when I'm working different types of situations, maybe a penalty kill or whatever, I want to know that the coach has the confidence to put me out there if that's what my role is going to be. We deal with it as players, but to be honest it's hard on everybody if all of a sudden you're not ever playing in the last few minutes of the game. That's an adjustment. You deal with it, and as a player you've got to respect the coach and do what he thinks is right, so it's a fine line.

How much of motivating the player is the coach's job, or does motivation need to come more from a player's initiative?

I think it comes from a player's initiative. Coaches can bring certain things to light and tweak the motivation based on statistics, like the fact you haven't scored in this barn, or you haven't scored against these guys in eight games, or something else you haven't thought about and you might not have thought about otherwise as a player, and it helps you get a little bit more motivated. However, I think the motivation should definitely come from within, and within the team. Having that goal and that pride of wanting to compete and be your best mostly comes from the player.

At the same time it's very important that coaches be like psychologists, because there is a certain way to get the most out of each player. They treat the players as a team, but players are also individuals.

How do coaches and managers build a winning environment?

It goes back to the roles you are going to have. Some guys have the role of playmaker, some will be goal scorers, some will be physical contributors, and some will be your tough guys. It is important to make everybody feel important but to also define their roles. I think that is a huge, huge deal. When roles are defined everybody takes pride in them.

And then coaches need to acknowledge those roles, too. If your fourth line doesn't play a lot but they can go out there and swing the momentum and have some big hits on another team's top line, acknowledge it so everybody feels important, everybody kind of gets their day. You don't want to be on a team where you feel you don't really matter. I think the motivation isn't there as much when you don't feel you really make a difference. So the best coaches make everybody feel like they make a difference, and they define their roles. That's a huge part of it.

Can players take away from a winning environment?

Yeah, I think that personalities are a big part of it. Games are tough. It gets physical and it gets emotional, and you don't want to be wasting energy as a group dealing with each other. We should all just focus on winning and being our best, because it can be draining if you know somebody isn't in it or doesn't care. It's rare, but you sometimes come across guys whose motivation you might question. It's rare, though.

When that happens do you try to fix it by talking to that person? If someone is taking away from this winning environment, how do you deal with that?

Part of it is trying to understand each other as players and teammates. Do they feel alienated; do they feel like they've got to look after themselves because nobody else will? I guess as a teammate you're trying to understand their motivation. Maybe they feel they're on the outside and they're either just temporarily going to be there or they're on their way out. You want to do your best to try to understand where they're coming from because in the end we play the game together. We all want to win, it's just that we might not go about things the right way and it might not have a positive effect on the team. You try to understand and adjust from there.

What motivates or drives you? Have you always had this drive, even as a youngster?

I think the motivation comes from competing to try to beat the team you're playing. But then you break it down: you're trying to beat the defenceman you're playing against, trying to beat the forwards, the other line. Just break it down in competition. I've always enjoyed scoring goals and getting points, even when I was really young, but at this time in my career, it's winning. I was very fortunate to be part of some winning teams in junior, World Junior, and the Olympics, but it's a pretty cool feeling when you look back as a group, and you think back to the hard times and think back to competing and how close it was, how it could have gone either way, and the sweat and the bruises and all that stuff, and how good it feels as a group to say we shared it with each other.

That's the best part of team sport: looking back on winning together. I made a lot of good friends that I still keep in contact with from junior because we won. I talk to my teammates over the years about their junior experiences, and they don't keep in contact with their teammates. I think part of the reason I did is because we won together and we have that special bond that winning creates. The biggest motivation now is definitely winning.

I thought I wanted to win before I got to the Stanley Cup final, but when you get that close . . . we were in the dressing room in Tampa Bay after the seventh game when we lost, and we could hear the different cheers and roars and we knew it was somebody else holding the Cup. Somebody else, when it could have been us. That was the toughest moment in sport for me for sure. To make my point, I thought I was hungry before, but it's much easier to get hungry now because it would be so nice to compare how great it would feel to win the Stanley Cup, to being on the bottom there.

What does "hungry" mean to you? That's such a great hockey word. "You've got a hungry team," or "he's a hungry player." What does that mean?

I think it's focus and determination. We always want to be good, but when you're hungry, it's a whole other level of focus and determination. When I'm playing my best, it's hard when the goals aren't going in and when I want to score a goal for the team, but I really feel I'm playing my best when I'm driving and competing and not thinking about the outcome and just going. It's another level of focus and determination.

How do you create team hunger?

There are little things that I've seen coaches do with statistics or articles about other players. Those types of things do bring a team together, as does just trying to imagine as a group how good it would feel to win or what you would do if you won. Also, just being more positive creates team hunger. You know it feels good to play as a team. When everyone has that confidence and a slight swagger, it's a good feeling as a team.

Having fun together is important, too, in creating that drive for the championship. Two years ago we were very close, and we had a lot of fun together and we enjoyed winning together. It's a balance. You don't want to be "loosey-goosey," but at the same time this is the time of our lives. The more fun we have together, the more I think you can find that little extra in a tough time, not only for yourself, but for each other.

How does raising the bar affect different people's hunger or expectations? You've been to the Stanley Cup final. Now next time back you expect to win. Does that create drive? Does that create hunger?

It's an adjustment. It's something different to deal with. Last year, especially early, we had a lot more expectations on our club because we had gone to the finals and for some of us who hadn't been through that before, it was an adjustment. You have expectations as a team and even personally. It's kind of that balance I'm still working on, trying to get ready in the right way and help fuel myself in the right way so that it's not a load or a burden, to try to enjoy it and not think of the outcome. I think as a team, and personally, finding balance is something that you definitely learn. I'm still learning to make sure I stay focused and not worry about whether I reach this or that or whether we reach this or that as a team.

What are the keys to your preparation for your best game?

I've noticed over the years, since I first started playing in the NHL, that when we played Edmonton, for example, I would be so excited to go in and play our big rival, the Oilers, in what always seemed to be big games in the standings against a team I had watched a lot growing up, that by the time the game started I would be burned out. I had no energy. I'm still working on keeping myself relaxed before a game. I find myself doing a little bit of thinking about the game during the day, but I play my best when I'm totally relaxed or when I try not to think about the game during the day. I try to keep my mind away from it and just try to be as relaxed as I can so that when the game time comes, I'm ready and I enjoy the competition and I'm not burned out. Once I'm at the rink, I start to focus on the game a little bit before warm up. I find that works best for me.

Take us through your preparation for the weeks and months leading up to the start of the season.

I believe in being in good physical shape and have always tried to improve my off-ice training over the years. It's helped me get a little bit quicker on the ice. I think that it's important to be in shape in order to give myself the best chance in the battles and to succeed. I take a few weeks off after the season from anything physical and then train during the summer and start gearing up. Early on in my career I tried to be in great shape for the first day of camp because that's when you're trying to make a good impression and you're trying to do well in the tests, but now I'm realizing as I get older that it's not really the first day of camp that's most important, it's the first day of the season. There's the luxury if you are a veteran. I think if you're a rookie and you're trying to make it, it's still important to make that good impression, but now I try to just gear up for the first day of the season, trying not to lose weight or strength.

How do you develop and maintain mental toughness?

I'm always reading about and working on that. Sometimes it's definitely stronger than others, and I think it's getting better. I've learned some things about myself over the years, but there are tough days, for sure. I enjoy reading different sports psychology and self-help books. Over the years I've talked to different sports psychologists. Last year I worked with Don Smith. This helps me get focused on the right things, because I can lose focus and worry about outcomes and results, rather than competing and concentrating on the process.

What are your favourite books so far?

My favourite book on mental preparation is *You Can if You Think You Can* by Norman Vincent Peale. I read that a couple of times and had great results in my play. I had my best runs when I was reading that. The book *Mind Gym* by Gary Mack with David Casstevans is also good.

Why is confidence so hard to put our finger on?

I think it's the most important thing. It's the difference between making that extra play, taking that extra time, or being hesitant out there. Hockey is a very fast game and once you get hesitant to play fast, you're getting checked. Confidence gives you that split second that makes a difference.

You're doing things at your pace as opposed to trying to react or being hesitant. I think guys are very, very skilled in the NHL, even more skilled than you see. From the first to the fourth line guys are very skilled, and I think part of what separates them is confidence. It's hard to explain why you have it or why you don't, but definitely some days you feel like you go in on a goalie and you can just see spaces and places where they were really no bigger than they were when you were having a tough time and didn't see anything.

Talk to us about the really confident times you've had as an athlete.

I had a 16-point game streak in my fourth year and ended up with 63 points. I played with Marc Savard and Andrei Nazarov. We were a confident line and we were having fun. Confidence and fun go together. If you're not confident, you're not having that much fun, or I'm not anyway, not nearly as much as I should be. It was a good streak, and I remember seeing that following the All-Star break I was right up there with Mike Modano and Jaromir Jagr for the most points. That was an eye-opener, and then I thought, "I wonder if I could get better and maybe be an elite player in this league?"

A big confidence breakthrough for me was when I got a late invite to the Olympic camp because someone was injured. I was probably the closest phone call and the guy that could get there in the shortest amount of time because it was in Calgary. I was very nervous to go, and I was a day late to the Calgary camp. It was in the summer. I showed up and skated with all the guys there and it was a huge confidence boost, not that I did anything spectacular or scored goals, but I felt like I held my own and didn't look out of place. That was a huge step and it was right before the season when I won the scoring race. It was a huge step going into the year thinking that maybe I would one day be an elite player. That made me believe it was possible.

I also remember when I was younger and struggling, I always wanted to get to the NHL. I always dreamed of playing in the NHL and being a star in the NHL. That's what I wanted to be, but I remember when I was younger and in my second year pro, wondering, just for a split second, if I was ever going to be a goal scorer in the NHL. Those were the tough times. The second year I had a tough year and ran into some injuries, and just all the way around it was a tough year. I've been very thankful that I've had the opportunity to score some goals, so there are definitely two different sides of confidence.

How important is character to being a high-performance player?

I don't know the actual definition, but when you say "character," what comes to mind—because I think we all have tough times and go through slumps and droughts and days where we don't feel as good both personally and with the team—is that willingness to fight through it and stick with it and keep working. In competition and in games where things are going to be very tough, you're either going to push back or you're going to wilt. I think that's the biggest thing, the more character you have, the more that you're willing to fight. It's not necessarily winning. I think it's being willing to give it everything that you have and to compete.

Can you remember a specific time that you were in a slump? If so, talk to us about how you broke out of it.

For whatever reason, I've had a lot of tough starts at the beginning of the year. I think part of it, as far as goals and scoring, is I put a little bit too much pressure on myself. Whenever I've stopped putting that pressure on—and it's hard to let go and trust that it will work out—I just relax a little bit and once again think about shooting the puck, skating, and getting to the net, as opposed to, "this game I'm going to score." When I put pressure on myself, I go in and say, "This is my chance, this is my chance to score," as opposed to just letting it flow. I think the best results just come when I relax. It sounds easy, but I just have to get back to thinking about what the process is and what my strengths are: shooting, skating, and getting to the net.

So again I'm hearing you say, "Focus on the process, not always the outcome."

I really do believe in that, but it's a lot harder to do. It's like growing up in minor hockey: you're scoring goals and you're having fun and you're just out there trying to do things. You're thinking about goals but you're not really. You're just enjoying yourself probably more than you are thinking, "I'm going to score." As the competition gets bigger it's important to keep that mind frame, but it's hard, and my best games, when I look back, were always when I really, truly enjoyed myself. It wasn't work. Maybe people would say I was working, but in my mind I was competing and just playing, just going out trying to do everything that I could, trying to win, trying to score, trying to beat the defencemen, all those things as opposed to working and thinking of the outcome.

That's a good point because so often coaches will say, "We're a hard-working team," but I always think they're all hard-working teams. I know what coaches are saying, but sometimes the contrast is what I'm hearing from some elite athletes like yourself: you've got to be in the zone more than you've got to outwork them.

I think so totally. To me, work seems, especially in the game, to be stressed too much. You want to do it, obviously, but I think that comes naturally. Think about kids again. If you watch kids play, they want to chase that puck as hard as they can and they don't think they're working. They want to go get that puck and they want to put it in the net and they want to score, but I don't think they think that's work. I think it's important for us as professionals to think that way, too, but it's hard. I want to enjoy myself all the time and relax and stay in the moment, but it's tough. It's tough when doubts start creeping in, and you start putting pressure on yourself as soon as you start thinking about outcomes. Once you start getting a little hesitant, it starts snowballing.

What is your greatest accomplishment so far, either with a team or personally?

As far as team accomplishments, the Olympics were very special. The final game was the most exciting game I've ever been in. It was a one-game final. When you're younger and you're on the rink and you imagine how games will be as you get older, that final game was *the* game as far as the passion in the crowd was concerned. It felt like half the crowd had their faces painted; half were Canadian and half were American. They were right into it. It felt like the fans were right on top of us, and you could feel their every emotion. I was nervous and I was excited. When I was on the ice I went as fast as I could. I didn't want to think about winning or losing until the last five minutes, when I think we scored and went up by two. We were actually going to win! It was the coolest game I've ever been a part of, and that was a pretty special experience. On a personal note, to win the scoring title and the goal title was special, and I'm thankful for that because you've got to have a lot of good breaks to do it. It's neat to think of the good times I've had over the years.

Let's move to adversity. What did it feel like to be traded, and how did you adjust to a new team?

I was traded before I got to the NHL. On one side I was thinking maybe Dallas didn't see what they'd hoped to see in me or maybe I wasn't living up to their expectations or they weren't as confident in me as I would have hoped. Then on the other side, after talking to Al Coates, the GM of Calgary, I understood that the teams were going in different directions and Calgary was excited about having me. I was excited about getting the opportunity to play in the NHL, but definitely my first few thoughts were that I hadn't met Dallas's expectations. But then you've got to just let that go. It definitely made it easier talking to the new GM who had traded for me. I had a lot of respect for Joe Neuwendyk, who went the other way in the trade, and realized what kind of player he was. I had to look at the positive side of it, that this other team saw a future in me.

What about personal adversity? What is your life plan for dealing with adversity?

Over the years my dad, my grandparents, and my mom have always been very positive people, and that had an effect on me. I like that. I think it's important to continue when things get tough, whatever they are. For my life, it's been hockey. It's important to work to stay focused and to keep trying to get better and to believe that things will get better—kind of creative anticipation. It's like the tide will come back. You had a drought, you believe it's going to change, you don't know when it will, but you expect it to, and you just keep doing everything positively that you can to help it and believe that it will, and it does. There have been some tough scoring droughts and some tough times being out of the playoffs as a team and losing games and things like that. I guess with the team, it's a little bit different. It's like a cycle. It feels tough at the time, but you know you're going in the right direction. The positive part is very important because everybody goes through droughts.

So it feels like the word might be "perseverance." How important is perseverance to your professional career, and how would you talk to a young person about it?

I think it's got to be one of the most important things in achieving your goals. Everybody has setbacks. One of my biggest ones was the bantam draft that we were talking about. Even while playing you have droughts. You don't really want them, but they help make you stronger, and they also help you appreciate the good times. If you always won everything you went into, you would never really appreciate winning. That's why I hope to win a Stanley Cup one day, and I tell you I'll appreciate it a lot more now after being that close and not winning.

What are the qualities of a closely knit team?

In my mind it's respecting different personalities. Some guys are quiet and some guys are vocal. You look at that and you accept it, having everybody feel that there's no hierarchy, there's no, "Well, I played more minutes so I get more say." We respect everybody and everybody has an equal voice and one guy is just as important as the next. It goes back to roles. Even if a player only plays for five minutes, it's not only the coach who acknowledges when he makes a big difference in a game, but also the players, as friends. When things are going tough, and we all go through tough times during our career, on and off the ice, I think it's important to pick each other up and find the positives in each other's games. Point it out and pat a guy on the back as opposed to ignoring him or giving him a kick.

How do teams build trust?

I guess you just believe your teammate's not going to do this or that at this time of the game. You've got to trust that everyone is doing their best. You want to see in the next guy beside you that we're doing our best, that we want to win and we're going to give it what we have and see where that goes, as opposed to, "I'm not trusting that anybody's not going to make a mistake." I guess it's big when you think about it. You're trusting that if you're giving everything you have, and it doesn't always go well, that your teammates are going to pick you up as opposed to put you down.

How about describing what your perception of a great team player is?

A great team player is someone who, when the games are on the line, not knowing what the outcome will be, more often than not is going to give it everything he or she has within his or her abilities. Some guys are great shot blockers, some guys are physical, some guys are more defensive, or whatever, but good team players are going to give it everything they have while competing. Also, a good teammate not only accepts his role but thrives in it and encourages his other teammates. It's easier to accept when a guy's playing 20 minutes, but for the guys who are playing 8 minutes and are positive about it, and negativity doesn't come through even though everyone wants to play more, those are great team players. That's probably one of the toughest roles, not to play a lot but still remain positive and be encouraging and be really good about your amount of ice time, because we all want to be good.

Have you ever had to put aside personal values to fit in as part of a team?

I think the closer teams do. Not everybody has the same personal values. We put importance on different things, and I think it goes back to respecting one another and accepting each other for who we are and looking for the good in one another as teammates. We can't all put the same importance in the same things, and we all have different opinions, whether political or religious, and I think it's important to have tolerance for one another.

When you were a young player who was your idol in hockey?

I had quite a few. I was an Oilers fan when I was growing up, and everybody loved Wayne Gretzky. That went without saying, but for me it was also Grant Fuhr. I loved his charisma and his energy, and being a black player, he really helped me in my career. Other black players, such as Claude Vilgrain and Tony McKegney, did, too. When I was growing up, a lot of kids asked me, "What are the chances you're going to make the NHL? There are no black players in the NHL." I was able to say, "What do you mean? There's Grant Fuhr. He's won Stanley Cups. He's an All Star. Claude Vilgrain scored 30 goals and Tony McKegney had 40 goals." It meant a lot to me to have something to say back, so I really looked up to those guys. I also looked up to Mark Messier. I loved his intensity and passion for the game, his fierceness.

How about memorable minor hockey memories? When you look back, what do you think of?

I think "fun." The most memorable were probably my Atom and PeeWee travelling teams. Some of my best friends are guys I played with when I was 10 or 11 years old. I guess the fondest memories aren't always on the ice. It's actually the camaraderie and the travelling and the hotels and playing ball hockey in the hallways or rug hockey. It's those memories that first come to mind, how much fun it was. I was very blessed to have a lot of good coaches who really emphasized fun and not so much work or dumping it in. We had good teams. We won provincial AAA a couple of times. Those were fun, but it was more the enjoyment of the game and camaraderie and the coaching staff finding ways to make practices fun.

So who most influenced your development?

My grandpa. My grandpa is into hockey. My parents divorced when I was very young. My dad went to school, and he was very busy, and my mom had to work very hard to get me into hockey. She made it to almost everything that I was in: baseball, hockey; she was a very busy lady. I really appreciate her efforts, but my grandpa and grandma were always there after school. I would go over and my grandpa would make sure my skates were sharpened and make sure I made it to practice at 4:00 because my mom would be working.

What I really appreciate most, when I look back, are their influences. My grandpa would be at every game and my mom would be at 99 percent of them, and when I came out it was always "Good game, good try." It was always positive; it was never "Oh, you didn't play well this game. You didn't work. You didn't go here or there." I really appreciate that, because I knew when I didn't play well. I wanted to play well; I wanted to score; I wanted to get as many points as I could, but I knew when I didn't play well. We had coaches to tell us if we were going to do this or that, so I really appreciated how they were almost passive. They were just there to enjoy it and support me. I went to lots of hockey schools, my grandpa got me into tons of hockey schools, but it was because I wanted to do it. It was his encouragement that really influenced me.

Who, living or dead, do you admire most in life?

Probably Martin Luther King, Jr. I admire everything he did for equality and how he probably knew he would get assassinated, but he was still courageous enough to keep fighting in a peaceful way. I admire just how brave and courageous and important he was.

If you could choose anybody to be your neighbour, who would it be?

I've always looked up to Michael Jordan. He was great as a basketball player. I love that he was also fearless. He was willing to try baseball. People said he would embarrass himself, but he didn't care. He wanted to do it because he wanted to do it. I really respect that, and that he wasn't afraid to fail.

If you hadn't played hockey or any other sport, what would you want to do and why?

I would probably be a lawyer. My dad's a lawyer. If you talked to my teammates they probably would say I enjoy debating too much. I just enjoy it. I enjoyed watching *Matlock*, growing up. I would probably be a lawyer.

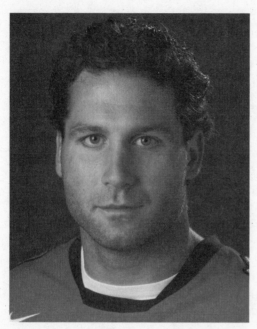

Ed Jovanovski

Windsor-born powerhouse defenceman Ed Jovanovski entered the NHL at the top, selected first overall by the Florida Panthers in 1994. The left-shooting defenceman then finished his junior career with his hometown Windsor Spitfires, where he was an OHL First Team All-Star, adding to his Second Team All-Star and All-Rookie Team Player status achieved the year before.

Jovo dove into the league with a big splash, trading southern Ontario for southern Florida. Despite the fractured hand he suffered in a pre-season game, he was named to the NHL's All-Rookie Team, was a Calder Cup Trophy finalist and was chosen Rookie of the Year by *The Hockey News* after advancing all the way to the Stanley Cup finals in his very first NHL season.

Ed Jovanovski became a Vancouver Canuck as part of the blockbuster Pavel Bure trade in January 1999. He played in three straight All-Star games in 2001, 2002, and 2003 and was named the Canucks' best defenceman for those same three seasons. Jovanovski, who didn't begin playing hockey until the age of 11, was named Canucks' assistant captain in October 2000. His strength, skating, and natural style played a major part in helping the Canucks set four new team records in 2002–03 for most points in a season (104), best road record, longest winning streak (10 games), and longest unbeaten streak (14 games), as well as a Northwest Division title in 2004.

Jovo's star has shone just as brightly in international play. He has won gold at the World Junior Championships (1995), the World Cup (2004), and the Olympic Games (2002). In between those events he represented Canada at an additional World Cup in 1996, winning silver, and at three World Championships.

Ed and his wife Kirsten have four children, Kylie, Kyra, and twins Cole and Coco. In addition to English, Ed speaks French and some Macedonian, courtesy of his professional soccer-playing father and mother, who immigrated to Canada from Yugoslavia. Ed Jovanovski signed a five-year deal with the Phoenix Coyotes in 2006 as an unrestricted free agent. He played in his fourth NHL All-Star game, as a Coyote, in 2007.

The Interview

Who were the best leaders you played with?

As a young player breaking into the league, I played with Brian Skrudland, who was my first captain in professional hockey. He wasn't the most skilled player on the ice, but his work ethic did the talking for him, and when he spoke everybody listened. I noticed that he always said something at the right time, because when he spoke he always hit the nail on the head. I was an 18- or 19-year-old kid listening to this guy who was 33. He was older, I knew he had won before, and it was amazing seeing him run that room. There were a lot of veterans on that team—Scott Mellanby, Mike Hough, Terry Carpenter, Gord Murphy, guys that had a lot of NHL experience— but the respect that they had for Brian was amazing.

What was the leadership quality he had that really stood out to you?

First, it was never pushing the panic button. I know from playing in Vancouver at times when things weren't going right, everyone got overwhelmed and started to panic. This guy was calm and cool. Whatever the issue was, he wouldn't care who you were. He would come out and say what he thought was needed, which involves walking a fine line in this game today, as it addresses accountability. If I was the captain and I had a guy like Mark Messier on my team, it would be tough for me to go say something to him, but Screwy didn't care who you were. He'd come up to you and give you constructive criticism or just tell you to "do this next time." He didn't care who the player was or how old he was; he just came out and said it. I think that's a really strong quality to have because sometimes you don't want to step on anyone's toes. We talked about this a lot when we were in Vancouver and it was hard for Markus [Naslund]. I think the game had changed so much that year that you didn't know what kind of response you were going to get back from a player if you said, "Hey listen, do it this way." Maybe the game has changed and it is more difficult to do that now, but I believe the ability to hold your guys accountable is an important quality to have as a leader.

How important is leadership within the room?

It's huge. In essence, you need 20 or 22 leaders, but you also need a backbone guy who is going to take charge in the dressing room. Whether he uses his words in the room or his actions on the ice depends on what kind of leader he is. I think you always need a captain who will step up and say something or take charge. If you look at football, the leaders are usually the quarterbacks and the strong defensive guys. I think hockey is the same way. You need your captain to be the boss.

What are your strongest leadership qualities?

I tend to never shut up before a game. I'm a vocal guy, and the biggest thing that I was taught was to be prepared all the time. When I say stuff in the room, it's all about starting the game, making sure we're ready at the beginning. This game is so hard if you get down a couple of goals. Obviously, I like to lead on the ice, and I like to play well every night. Whether it's going good or bad, I want to make sure our guys are on their toes and ready to play.

Not all players wear an "A" or a "C," but how important are those glue guys on the team?

They're really important. Like I said earlier, hopefully there are 20 leaders on the team. It's just as important that everybody is on the same page. You can't have one guy deviate from the system. If the players see that, it's deflating for a team. One guy may play three minutes and another guy 30 minutes, but we need equal leadership from each and every guy doing his part.

Pick out a couple of NHL coaches that you've enjoyed playing for and tell us what you've respected about them.

I started my career with Dougie McLean, who was perfect for a new team. He hadn't had much experience, but his intensity and his emotion for the game really carried over to the passion and intensity I have for the game. Marc Crawford is probably the best coach I've had in my career, just because he knows how to get the best out of his players. He'll challenge his top guys and the guys that don't play that much to get to that opportunity where they do play. During my first couple of years with Marc, he challenged me every day, and I feel I'm a better player for it. His preparation and organizational skills are top shelf. He and his assistants, Mike Johnston and Jack McIlhargey, worked very well together in Vancouver. I think Crow is one of those very demanding coaches who's won before and knows what it takes to win, so you have to respect that part of it, and trust in what he's doing. When he's on you and when he wants more out of you, essentially he wants to make you a better player.

What was different in Crawford's approach from, say, Wayne Gretzky's approach in Phoenix?

Wayne is definitely a guy who has played the game at an elite level, and to see him in the coaching role is a little weird for a player like me who grew up idolizing him. I've never seen a guy who wants to win more than Wayne does. We were down once 4–1 to Atlanta, and when we scored the fourth goal to come back in the game, he almost jumped into the stands. His care for his players stands out, and he is very approachable for a guy who has done everything on the ice and has won so much before. I think what really bothers the guy is when we're not playing well for him. He almost puts his hands up in the air and thinks, "What can I do better?" The next day he'll have a bunch of video for us, and it almost looks like he hasn't slept the night before. I think as he is getting more into coaching since his second year, he's developing into a guy who really cares about his players and just has one thing on his mind, and that's helping players along.

Ed, you've described three very different coaches. What are some of the qualities that you've responded to in a coach?

Any time I'm challenged I feel that I respond and play my best hockey. Marc telling me that I had more to give and trying to get the most out of my abilities on the ice helped me. Marc is really good at doing that and getting that out of his players. As a player you want to go out and play well, and you're following guidelines from the coach.

How much of motivating the player is the coach's job, or does most of it need to come from the player?

I think it has to come from the player, but it also comes from the coaches. Sometimes a coach gives you a speech, and you're ready to run through the wall to get to the ice, but I think a higher percentage of the time motivation comes from inside yourself. You've got to be prepared and mentally ready to go out there and perform.

How do you like to be communicated to as a player, pushed or patted on the back?

When I broke into the league I was treated differently. Every coach realizes that you don't want to get on a young player too much because there's the possibility of the player shutting it down and not being able to take it. Now, later on in my career, I definitely can accept the yelling and the criticism along with the positive stuff. I respond better to being challenged, and I don't expect anyone other than my teammates to pat me on my back. Coaches expect that out of their top guys, and when things aren't going well you're the first one to hear it, so for me it's always a challenge. I want to be better, I want to help my teammates, and I'll leave it at that.

How do you build a winning environment?

I think you do research on guys you want to bring into your locker room; you draft well. You hear all the time you want character guys, and you want to have that fine balance of your skilled guys and your glue guys, your muckers, and you definitely need strong goaltending. I would say some of it could be a little luck, too. If you find a gem in the rough and it pans out for you, it's great.

When you have a dressing room that is not quite as strong, the environment's not where it needs to be, how, as a player, do you change that?

As players you look at the reason why things aren't going right. You try to make corrections. You always can work harder; you always can give a bit more effort. I think that's all players can do. If we look in the mirror and ask, "Are we giving it our best?" and we can't say "Yes," then maybe there needs to be a shakeup in the dressing room. I think that for the most part if everybody is buying into the system and everybody is pulling on the rope the same way, you usually win your games. That's a perfect scenario of what went on with our team one season. At the start of the year it was miserable. It turned into a job. It was like we didn't care how much money we were earning, it was tough getting up and going to the rink every day because it was miserable. We were losing, 10, 15 games under .500, and I think everybody finally realized that it wasn't going to get better unless it was corrected in the room, and it started with us. I think everybody took a long, hard look in the mirror and said, "I can give that 10 percent more."

At the end of the day, Eddie, what drives you, what motivates you as a player?

It's the big picture, winning that Stanley Cup. Not too many people are fortunate enough to get it. I have been paid very well since I was 18 years old, so it's not a financial issue that's driving me, it's going out there and being the best in my position and helping my team win, and winning the Stanley Cup. I would retire a very happy man if I win a Stanley Cup. That's all I play for.

How do you sustain that hunger as a player?

I look at it that there's not anything in the world I'd rather be doing. Playing hockey is a childhood dream of mine. I'm 30 years old and I've been doing it for 12 years, and every day that I go on the ice and skate around I think, "What else would I rather be doing than playing a game I love on a big stage and having a chance to win a Stanley Cup?" You know, that drives me every day.

How about team hunger? How do you keep a team hungry?

Everyone has to have the same goal. If I asked every teammate, "Why are you playing this game?" I think they'd say, "The opportunity to win a Stanley Cup." You keep a team motivated and hungry by winning. I can't wait to get on the ice tomorrow night. We're winning, and we want to be out there.

Walk us through the way you prepare for games. Pick your best game and tell us how you prepared for it.

I prepare the same way whether I have a good one or a bad one. I try to prepare the same way every game. I skate every day, do our meetings and go for my meal. I get to the rink a few hours before the game, and I start thinking about what I've got to do to be good that night. I study the game sheets that are given to me, and once I start lacing up the skates I really start focusing. I still get nervous, to this day, going onto the ice. There's that part of me that keeps it exciting. I don't do anything special, but I do focus and prepare to be my best, and that's about it.

What about preparation in the months, weeks, and days leading up to a season? Is there anything you do specifically that you can pass on to kids reading this?

I think this game has turned into a 12-months-of-the-year commitment where you take a few weeks off right after the season. I think it depends on how old the kids are, but all kids should be introduced into sports other than hockey throughout the summer. That's my feeling on it. I think professionals just want to do everything necessary to be prepared for the season. Make sure you're healthy going into the season. Make sure you are in the best possible physical shape you can be in, because it's a long grind. It can mentally challenge you. It depends how the year is going, but I think it's a long process. You just want to be prepared for what's going to happen.

How did you develop your mental toughness?

I think just by trial and tribulation in the game. I've played in some very big games in my career, and I've lost some very big games. I think that builds mental toughness, not succeeding. Not succeeding and then finally getting over that hump gives you a positive outlook and makes you that much stronger down the road. I'm not talking just hockey, I'm talking life in general.

Why is it so hard to put our finger on confidence?

It's kind of like a teeter-totter. You hear how this guy is soaring with confidence or this guy is lacking in confidence, but I think when things are going well I've tried to remain in the middle and not get too high, and when things are going down not to get too low. Personally I don't know exactly how to describe confidence, but I know confidence is something that you get through working hard. You work hard and at some point you're going to reap the benefits of that and you'll turn into a confident guy, but, as you know, this game is very humbling, team-wise and individually. You can start very well and kind of tail off. Like I said, it's kind of like a teeter-totter. Confidence is a tough word to describe, even though you hear it all the time.

Give us your most exciting moments as an athlete.

I think just having the opportunity to be drafted and play a game in this league was exciting for me. It's a childhood dream. Then playing in

All-Star games, the Olympics, and Stanley Cup finals were all special moments that I'll cherish. Playing in the Stanley Cup finals and the Olympics is, I think, the pinnacle of where an athlete can be, and I experienced winning a gold medal. It was a pretty joyful experience.

How important is character to being a high-performance player?

It's really important. I think you almost have to tie in the words selfish and selfishness to character. Character guys are not selfish players. They care about their teammates. They care about their surroundings. They care about how the team is doing. It's always team first; character guys all have that quality. I've played with a lot of character guys who really care about the game and care about the team and respect the process, and I've played with guys who didn't care. I'm sure everybody's experienced that kind of selfishness, and you can't fool the players. The players know who they are, and they know what you're all about. There are definitely more character guys than not in this league.

What are some of the setbacks you've experienced? More important, how do you rebound? How do you become the elastic person that you need to be?

We all face adversity, whether it's in our personal life or in the game. In the game I've had some unfortunate injuries the past couple of years, and it's always tough when you face that. You want to get healthy and you want to get back to help the team, and all you can do is just kind of stay focused on what's in front of you. If it's adversity through a losing stretch, we correct it by working harder and finding a solution to what's going on. Ultimately, you rebound through hard work. If you beat the guy next to you and your teammates do that as well, you're going to win most nights. If you run into a very hot goaltender, you can accept those losses.

Personally, we lost a baby, and I remember that being a very tough time for me. Sometimes you're dealt those times that you don't want to deal with, but if you have strong people around you to help, you get through it. With my teammates and the support from the organization, we all got through it.

I wish we talked about this more, not only for kids, but also young pros. How did you adjust to being traded, and how did you adjust to your new team? Walk us through some of the feelings you had and what you did to make it happen.

I remember clear as day, my wife and I were hanging a tapestry in the kitchen when the phone rang. It was Brian Murray telling me that he traded me to Vancouver. I remember the next morning I had a 6:00 a.m. flight. At this time Kylie was only seven months old. I remember getting on a flight the next morning, leaving the house to catch my 6:00 flight, and playing that night in Dallas. I remember my dad telling me, "I'm so proud of you. You're 21 years old and you're moving not only to a new city, but to another country." I think everyone realizes it's a part of the game and teams try to do this to better their own teams. I think it made me mentally stronger, as well, knowing that you can change cities and you can adjust and things will work out just fine. They did for me in Vancouver. I loved it there, and I really miss it.

Your point is well taken that the younger you are as you go through that, the more prepared you are to go through it again.

I think having already gone through it at an early age, when I was approaching free agency in Vancouver, I kind of knew what to expect if I was switching destinations. It made it a lot easier having gone through something like that before.

How about pressure, Eddie? How do you like to handle pressure?

I really enjoy it. I was saying to some people in Phoenix that you miss the daily pressures of playing in the Canadian market, playing in Vancouver. Obviously Vancouver's a hockey hotbed, and I learned better than ever in that city that as a player you want to go out there and you want to put your best foot forward. For me, the primary pressure was the pressure I put on myself to be the best that I could possibly be. I had coaches who pushed me but never put that added pressure, kind of like an ultimatum, on the player, and I felt I played my best hockey under those circumstances.

I think you're saying the same thing Sakic and Iginla both said when talking about pressure. You said that you love it, and I used to be that way. They both said that during pressure situations they try to get calmer. Isn't that interesting?

Yeah, those guys are prolific goal scorers. I think as a defenceman you really need to know your surroundings, know the situation, and just try to eliminate that pressure and try to get it done, whatever which way you can. Obviously in the game itself, there's pressure. I don't think extra added pressure is going to be beneficial to the player. I think you need to block everything out when you are on the ice.

Chemistry—what are the qualities of a closely knit team?

I kind of touched on this before. Everybody having the same goals is huge; everybody trying to focus on the same thing and knowing what it's going to take to accomplish it. You hear all the time people talking about defence pairings or forwards that have chemistry together on the ice. I think that's a small piece of chemistry, but I also think there's got to be chemistry away from the game. I think doing things together on the road builds chemistry and that gets transferred into the locker room and then onto the ice.

Pat Quinn's big word was "trust." How important is trust to a team?

Huge, along the same line as accountability. Trust is a powerful word. If I know the guy next to me is doing his job, then I know I can concentrate on my job and vice versa. I think trust in one another can take you a long way.

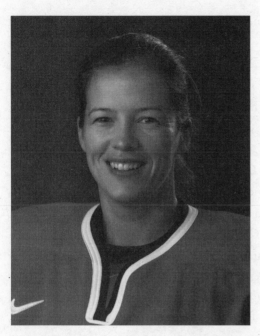

Cassie Campbell

How many Canadian women, or any women for that matter, have won three Olympic medals, modelled on the cover of a national magazine and replaced Harry Neal on *Hockey Night in Canada*? Cassie Campbell has done all that and more since she donned her first pair of skates at age five. She was born in Richmond Hill, Ontario, played girls' hockey in Brampton, collegiate hockey at the University of Guelph and professional hockey in Mississauga, Toronto, and Calgary, but all of Canada claims this National Women's Hockey Team hero as their own.

An all-round athlete, Cassie was named Peel's Most Valuable Player in the north division as a member of the Peel Champion North Park Secondary School girls' basketball team in 1991. While earning a degree in honours sociology, Cassie focused on hockey and helped the Women's Hockey Gryphons win the Ontario Women's Intercollegiate Athletic Association Gold medal in 1995. In 1996 she won the University of Guelph's W.F. Mitchell award, presented annually to a graduating student who has demonstrated outstanding talent and ability in a sport, as well as exceptional leadership and involvement in athletics.

Cassie joined the Women's National Hockey Team in 1994 and was named its captain at the start of the 2001–2002 season. Over the ensuing 13 years she won 21 medals in international and Olympic competition, including 17 gold and 4 silver. She has taken part in three Winter Olympic Games and has the distinction of being the only captain, male or female, to have led Canada to two Olympic Gold Medals. In addition, she represented Canada in seven International Ice Hockey Federation World Women's Championships, nine Four Nations Cups, and the Torino Ice Tournament. The 1996 World Championship "all-tournament all-star" amassed 100 points in 157 career games.

In October of 2006, Campbell made history by becoming the first female colour commentator for *Hockey Night in Canada*, having previously joined the program as a rinkside reporter following her retirement from professional hockey in August of 2006. She also covers all female Hockey Canada events for TSN and was recognized in 2006 as one of Canada's Top 20 Most Influential Women by the Canadian Association for the Advancement of Women and Sport and Physical Activity. In 2006 Campbell was named the *Toronto Sun* Sportsperson of the Year, and in 2007 she was inducted into both the Alberta Sports Hall of Fame and the Canadian Sports Hall of Fame.

Cassie Campbell has continuously worked toward the betterment of the sport and the betterment of all. She is a spokesperson for the Chevrolet Safe and Fun Hockey Program, runs an annual street hockey tournament that raises over $200,000 a year for Ronald McDonald House in Southern Alberta, is a spokesperson for Health In Perspective (a Health Canada initiative dedicated to preventing young girls from smoking) and is a Calgary Olympic Development Association board member.

Now a polished motivational speaker, Cassie is also the author of two books released in October 2007: *Some Things I've Learned: Lessons on Motivation, Passion, Excellence and More* and *H.E.A.R.T*, co-written with Lorna Schultz Nicholson. Current Team Canada captain Hayley Wickenheiser has said of her former teammate: "Cassie was a tenacious two-way player, a good skater and forechecker. Mind you, she also did a lot of singing and dancing around the dressing room; she was definitely our team's best candidate for *Canadian Idol*." For Cassie Campbell, this is probably not a stretch!

The Interview

Walk us through your hockey background and development.

I started playing hockey on an organized team when I was seven years old, but I had the skates on when I was three, on the pond. With the exception of two years of my career, I played pretty much with girls. I captained the University of Guelph team, where I was fortunate to have been coached by Sue Shear, the first captain ever of the World Championship team. I started playing with the national team in 1994, as captain from 2001 to 2006, and have won six World Championships, one silver medal, and two Olympic gold medals.

Who were the best leaders you played with, and what were the qualities that made them the best?

The best leaders I ever played with really had a good awareness of the team and, obviously, what they did on the ice. They were not necessarily the goal scorers on the team, but people who were willing to do whatever it was going to take to win. Whether it was playing on the first line or the fourth, or killing a power play, it didn't matter. They worked hard no matter what role they were in. You could really tell they put the team before their own successes, put themselves on the line every time they were on the ice, and worked hard off the ice; they were probably the most fit on the team. Frances Louis and Stacey Wilson, who were former captains of the national team, really stand out to me as top-notch leaders of our program.

Did you have different expectations of leaders prior to joining the national team, or were you surprised and excited with what you saw in these leaders?

I think having grown up watching them play prior to my making the team, I had definitely put them on a pedestal, and those two didn't disappoint. There have been others I have put on a pedestal, and then had a chance to meet, with whom I have been really disappointed. Frances and Stacey didn't disappoint. Their work ethic was second to none. They were there for the team, and I really wanted to try and emulate them as much as I could.

What were the characteristics and values that you wanted to emulate?

Work ethic, first and foremost, and the ability to be a two-way hockey player. Both of them were that way. They took as much pride in blocking shots as they did in scoring goals. They also had good team awareness. I always tried to be there for my teammates when they needed me. I was sort of one of the ones the younger players came to, and I didn't feel good about this, but I think Frances and Stacey brought a lot of perspective. I'm a big-picture thinker; I don't allow a lot of little things to fester and become big things. I try to get people to look at the big picture.

How long did you wear the "C" for the national team? Take us in the dressing room a little bit. From your perspective, how important is leadership in the room and is that where it evolves first?

I was a captain or assistant from 1997 to 2006 on the national team and captain of my club teams and my university team, so I've been pretty fortunate. Important leadership is in the room. You spend so much time in the dressing room and off the ice together, so I think that off-ice component of leadership is also really valuable. You have the ability to impact and say positive things to people every day. Maybe not to every player on a daily basis, but you have a chance to make a positive statement to at least one person. It's important as a leader to do that. People want to feel appreciated not only on, but also off the ice. Sometimes I think if they feel appreciated off the ice, then they will perform better on the ice. Leadership within the dressing room is essential because it can make or break a team. If you're not together in the dressing room, chances are you're not going to be together on the ice.

One of my favourite authors, Os Guinness, once said that culture is created by three things: what we affirm, what we confront, and what we demonstrate. Take us into your leadership style. How did you work those three things out?

I think people know that I'm real. They knew it was difficult for me to say the hard things, but they also knew I was doing it for the betterment of the team. They knew that I was there for them, and I didn't pretend to be better than anyone else. I just tried to make sure that people knew I was equal to them and that they were a huge part of the team and just as important, even if they didn't have a "C" or an "A." I guess I demonstrated that on the ice by just working hard and buying into the systems and if there was a time to put my body on the line, doing it. I'm not going to say I was the one who was going to score that big goal, but I would definitely have something to do with it, whether it was making the pass or being in on the forecheck. Despite the profile I've gotten recently from playing hockey, I really tried to share it with the women's game. I tried to get things for my teammates, like sponsors, for example. I don't necessarily like being in the public eye, but I can use publicity to help the game.

Talk to us about other players on the team who are not in overt leadership positions but are key glue gals. How important are they and, as a leader, how did you work with them?

I remember telling Mel Davidson, prior to the 2006 Olympic year, that I really thought we needed to let other people know that they were leaders. Hayley Wickenheiser, Vicky Sunohara, and I had been captains and assistants for two Olympics by then, and sometimes people looked to us to do the leading when, really, we might have needed help from some of the other girls on the team. Maybe the younger players were afraid to step up, so we brought two other players, Karen Ouellete and Cheryl Pounder, into the group. By including them in all the leadership meetings and asking for their input on many things, I think we helped them to feel that they were leaders and should contribute in that fashion. Those two played tremendously for the team and really stepped up into the leadership role. It was good for us to allow them to feel part of it—to let them in. I think we always look to our "C"s and "A"s to lead, and that's where we really miss the boat. You don't have to wear a letter to be a leader.

What do you respect most about the coaches you played for? What things stand out from your player's perspective?

It's been difficult in the female game, over the years, to find coaches who are technically strong, who know what they're talking about. Mel Davidson is technically strong, and therefore we trusted the things that she brought to the table. Good coaches are passionate and admit when they make mistakes. They are not afraid to single someone out or send a wake up call. They are not afraid to do that to the first line centre as well as the seventh defenceman. They treat everyone equally. You can't always do that, but for the most part a good coach does.

It is also important for a coach to be a great communicator. Both Danielle Sauvignon and Melanie Davidson were really good communicators. After we went through a tough Olympic year, losing eight times to the Americans, Danielle listened to things I had to say about the team and was open to new ideas. It wasn't the coaches who stood up and thought they were the power and the ones winning all the medals, but the coaches who appreciated their team and their players who were my favourite coaches.

How did the coach get the best out of you? Did you need a pat on the back; did you need a kick sometimes? Walk us through how the coaches got the best out of you.

I loved to have a coach in my face and challenging me. I didn't like coaches who "kissed my butt," so to speak. I liked to be challenged and learn different things. I was open to the opportunity of having a coach who could teach me at the latter stage of my career, and every once in a while I needed a kick in the butt. I always appreciated being challenged. I respected someone who communicated well and was open and honest and didn't beat around the bush. Just tell me how it is; this is what I've got to do. "This is why you are playing on this line today, and if you don't like it, that's it." I always enjoyed playing for someone like that.

How much of motivating the player is the coach's job, and how much comes from the player?

I think the coach has to step into the dressing room and say the right things at the right time, but I definitely believe motivation comes from within, especially when you are talking about our national team. You're playing for your country, and if you can't motivate yourself then you probably shouldn't be there. I do think a coach has the obligation to step up and say the things that may be needed to motivate a team, more so than an individual.

What is a winning environment and how do coaches build it?

The Olympic year in 2006 was a perfect winning environment. We started off with what was essentially a three-week boot camp. From a team perspective, I think there was nothing we were going to face that was going to be as hard as that. From there on in we knew it was going to be easy.

In previous years leading up to the Olympics, we trained so much but played maybe 20 games, and you really don't bring out the best in each other doing that. The 2006 Olympic year was better because we had played 54 games by February, more than any NHL team at that point. You're going to be successful as a hockey team if you play challenging games. We were down 3–1 going into the third period in some of these games and were able to come back. Those are the types of things that build the character and team chemistry that you need in order to win. We also worked hard off the ice; there was no one who skimped out on workouts.

A lot of us, especially the older players, had our roles change over the years, but you could tell all of us accepted them. After losing in 2005 everyone really bought into the program and would do whatever it was going to take to win. We had a good balance of workouts, team-building activities, and games. I thought we had a good awareness of each other and really knew each other and were more professional because of it. That, to me, is a winning season.

The one thing that is clear with Canadian teams internationally is the expectation that it's gold or bust. How much of that drives a winning environment?

I think it's huge. For years you've seen other sports in Canada whose players are satisfied just to compete at the Olympics, and now you're seeing those players say they want to win medals. Winning a medal in some of these sports is like a gold medal in hockey for Canada. Canadian hockey players are born and bred both wanting to win and accepting nothing but winning, willing to do whatever it takes to win. We don't accept anything but gold, and we also appreciate and understand how difficult that medal is to attain and how precious those winning moments are.

Once you have a winning environment, can one or two players ruin it?

They can if you let them. As much as our team had a perfect season in 2005–06, you still have those people (I call them high-maintenance) who really think they are leaders but are not. The challenge is somehow incorporating them so they continue to believe they are leaders and putting them in a position in the team setting where no matter what happens they'll come out as leaders. I think that there are certain people that you have to coax and coddle along to keep them on the positive side of things, but you never let on that you're doing that. There are definitely people you are constantly aware of—what's going on with them, who they're talking to, and the conversations they're having with people. As leaders on our team, everything always came back to us.

Steve Yzerman, who has always been one of my favourite players of all time, told me a story about a player he and Brendan Shanahan played with in Detroit. He was such a good player that they took him out for dinner, just to make him feel like he was part of it. I think there are people you need to do that with. They are such good players that you need them on your team, and you have to spend the extra time with them.

What motivated you? Have you always had that drive even through your younger years?

I guess just the love of the game. It sounds like a cliché, but I think to be successful at something and to work as hard as we do, you have to love it and that love has to come from within. I've always wanted to win at any level I've ever played, in bantam in a Mississauga tournament, or going to Guelph and winning the Ontario or Canadian Interuniversity Sport (CIS) Championship. Everything was about winning to me. I couldn't care less who scored the goals, it was just about winning. That motivated me. I know you might not want to share that with the kids because it's not always about winning—it's about the memories—but for me, playing an elite level of hockey, there's no question: it was about winning.

I coached minor hockey for 15 seasons with our three boys and have always struggled over the importance of winning in minor sport. I've changed my opinion. The game is about winning, but we are trying to teach kids how to win and lose with the right attitude.

Looking at our Olympic experience, without our loss in the '98 Olympics, we wouldn't have had the later success. You don't want to tell people to be happy to lose, but you want to tell kids that you learn from losing; those are the moments you learn the most from. When you're winning, everything is great, but when you're losing, you really have to look at what was done wrong, not only by yourself but, obviously, by the organization. You learn most about yourself in these situations. After '98, for sure I knew what I could have done better. I think it's okay to tell kids to win, but you also have to tell kids it's okay to lose if you look at it from a winning perspective. Even if you're winning, that doesn't mean you're having fun, so I think it's important to make sure you have fun along the way too, and take some time to step back and enjoy what's going on.

I frequently say that the difference between winning and second place is to have that "hungry spirit." How did you develop your hungry spirit and help maintain your team's hungry spirit?

As I got older in my career, I went through more moments where I wasn't as hungry as I was in my younger days. Part of it was overcoming injuries. My hunger to go back to win the 2006 Olympics was because no other country had won two gold medals in women's hockey, and I wanted to be part of the team that was the first. You set new goals; some of them are big and some of them are small. I wanted to get better at some part of my game every year. One year I hired a shooting coach and another, focused on my skating. You build hunger by just trying to do new things.

To keep the team hungry I tried to share the leadership more and show how passionate I was about this. I looked at leadership in three different cycles. The first one was learning how to be a leader. The second cycle was when I was the leader and had to get the job done. The third cycle, as my career wound down, was letting other people lead and making sure that I was leaving some sort of legacy by showing them my passion and hunger for the game. I also felt I could bring out other people's hunger and passion by allowing them to step up and lead and show them that they are appreciated.

Would you agree that purpose and passion drive our hunger, and could you give us an example of how that was perpetrated in your life?

After winning in the 2002 Olympics, I went through a lull in my hockey career. We had been on such a high that it was almost like a post-Olympic depression. It sounds crazy, but it's quite a real phenomenon. I stopped making goals. I was sort of playing but really just going through the motions, and for a year I just didn't have any real goals. It was like, what do I do now? What more can I do? It took me a good six months before I started to reinvent my wheel of goals. I had been complacent, stuck in a rut, then I asked myself, "Cassie, what do you need to do better as an athlete, and, from a team perspective, what do we need to do better?" I became more involved in the behind-the-scenes planning of the year, and I wanted to be part of it. Those new goals brought back the passion of the game.

How did you prepare for the best games you played?

I didn't really like to think about the game too much before playing. Getting a good rest and good food and a coffee were important to me. I liked to be loose. I played my best games when I was loose in the dressing room, listening to music and just sort of having fun, maybe playing hacky sack or soccer before the game. My best game was when I was enjoying everything.

Going onto the ice I became more focused on mental preparation. I really did smell the ice, and I tried to skate certain ways during warm up—quick strides so it felt like it was a flowing motion. I liked to handle the puck just a little bit when I was standing in line, and there was lots of talk from me, lots of communication. All these things brought the best game out of me.

How did you prepare coming into a season? What were the things you would do during the months prior to the start of your season?

Obviously, physical training was a big part of it for me. The last month

before my season began was about explosiveness and being fast. One of my weaknesses as a player was lacking quick reaction and explosiveness, so I worked on those things for the last month and got them embedded in my brain and my nerves.

There was also something I learned later. Sometimes we get so caught up in all the things we have to do to get better—like stickhandling, skating, and training off the ice—that we forget about rest. This is something that I didn't understand in the earlier stages of my career. I played for two teams seven nights a week, plus training. It was crazy. Now that I am older, I realize what rest is and that taking a day off from training is probably more important than the training itself.

Kids are playing so many sports and doing so many different things. Some of them now are playing hockey exclusively, and I don't necessarily think that's a healthy thing. I believe playing other sports, like soccer, makes you a good hockey player because of its fitness aspect and because it helps you to become more athletic.

For me, it was about explosiveness during that later part of the summer leading into the season. I wasn't one of the bigger players building muscle mass. Trying to maintain a certain weight during the season was always tough, so that last month was the hardest, getting all those things where they needed to be.

Describe how you built your mental toughness.

I wasn't one to watch a lot of video, but if I felt that I'd played a bad game, rather than dwelling on it, I'd go and watch the game right away. If I thought it was the worst game I'd ever played, after watching the video, I would realize things weren't so bad. I kept a journal of different things I learned along the way. I think writing things down was sort of my release, getting things out of my system.

My mental toughness came from a team perspective: we're going to war this year and I've got to show up every day. That's sort of the mentality I had. My weakness may have been forgetting to look at the individual things I could have done to be tougher mentally because I based everything so much on the team part of it: as long as I showed up every day. It wasn't until later in my career that I realized that I should look at the mental side of the game and how it could help to make me better.

Parking things was always a big thing for me, and I eventually learned to do that. I remember in my rookie year I played defence with a French girl who could only say, "Park it." I made a bad pass and came off and she immediately said, "Park it." So what, you made a bad pass. I mean, you watch the NHL, it happens. I became really good at allowing things to just sort of roll off my back. Maybe I could have worked more on the mental side, but I didn't find that was part of me.

Talk to us about the elusive word "confidence"; in sport we talk about it a lot. What is confidence to you, and how did you continuously build it?

I think a lot of players lose their confidence if they don't get points. Points are such a big thing, and yet there is so much more to a hockey game. You might have made that first initial breakout pass and you don't get an assist, but it was critical to the goal. I always understood and tried to appreciate the little things everyone, including me, did and tried to celebrate those things as much as possible. That sort of helps you keep your confidence, but it's a fragile thing. My confidence would come and go. Whenever I felt I lost confidence, I would address it the next day in practice. If my hands just didn't feel good the night before, I worked on it, but I didn't base my confidence on scoring or points. I just knew there was so much more to my game.

After some of my best games, the coaches have said, "Gosh, that was the best game you've ever played. You didn't get any points, but you were all over the ice and making things happen." Sometimes the puck just doesn't go in. I think every athlete goes through the up and down process. It's about finding the right person you can talk with to get things off your chest, or watch video, or just work a little harder in practice on something that you didn't feel so confident about.

Can a coach take away or give you confidence?

I definitely think coaching decisions play a big part in your confidence. If you're on the power play and then for one shift you're not, for some reason, your confidence can drop. With different coaches your role changes, too, and that also plays a part in your level of confidence. If with one coach you're always on the first line and with the next coach you're on the third, it has an effect. But I still think it's up to the athlete to perform to the best of their ability under any circumstance. A couple of the girls that were cut in my last year were first- and second-line players on their club teams, but when you come to the national team that's not the way it's going to be. The people who were confident and played different roles made the team. I do think the coach can have an impact, but ultimately it comes down to the athlete and their confidence.

Can a coach or a leader take that hungry spirit away from a player?

I think so. A coach who doesn't appreciate third- and fourth-line players can destroy a team. When it comes down to crunch time, obviously you need your goal scorers to score, but you also need your role players to step up and step up big. If the role players see the superstars go out there and not backcheck, not block shots, not do those team things and still get the ice time, it really can take away from what I think could be the character and the heart and soul of your team. This is especially true in a long season. In the NHL, it ultimately comes down to making the playoffs and winning the Stanley Cup. In our case, the goal was to get to the World Championships or the Olympics. As a coach, you really need to make sure that you show appreciation for the role players. In most cases, the hunger comes from character guys and two-way type players.

In my last year with Mel, every line and every person was appreciated. I think that's why we played so well as a team. Although we scored so many goals, they weren't end-to-end rushes. There were five people touching the puck, sometimes the goalie made the save, and then it went up the ice and resulted in a goal. Everyone was appreciated.

Everyone understood her role and she adjusted accordingly as different things happened.

Can you pick out one of your most exciting moments as an athlete?

What stands out is winning the Ontario University Championship with Guelph in 1995. I was the only national team player on the team. At that time we had a bunch of no-name players and a lot of girls from small towns who didn't grow up with great coaching. We struggled all year. We were never in first place, always in third or fourth, and we beat a team in the final that had nine national team players. They were by far the favourite team, but we beat them because we were a better team. People bought in and worked hard and improved over the year. The girls who came from small towns and didn't necessarily have great hockey sense learned a lot and improved on their weaknesses. By the end of the year we had the complete package.

2002 was another big year for me because a lot of things happened to our team that could have destroyed us. We had eight losses to the United States, which is never fun for a Canadian hockey player. We had a key injury one week before going to the Olympics, and that person was replaced by a younger player. There were things that just tore our dressing room apart. As one of the leaders trying to keep that team together who was emotionally exhausted by the end of it, that stands out for me as a great accomplishment from a team perspective. Knowing what I had to do behind the scenes, it was one of my worst years in hockey, but one of my best years as far as being the best leader I knew how to be.

How important is character, and how would you describe a character player on your team?

Character is key. A goal scorer who is able to go in the corners and be physical shows character to me. The fourth-liner who sits on the bench, and steps up and is excited, shows character. I remember a game in 2002 where we had so many penalties called against us. We had five really key players as far as offence and power play goes who sat on the bench the whole game because they weren't on the penalty kill. They just moved down the bench and let the penalty killers take their spot, and that's character: being willing to sacrifice their individual goals for the team's sake. I don't think character is something you teach; you either have it or you don't.

So you've got to look for character, find it in the players you want to have on your team?

I think so, although I think sometimes you have to give up character for offensive capabilities. The reality is hockey is about scoring goals, but if you have the character around that portion of your team, you'll be fine. I remember Steve Yzerman, being that great offensive player that he was, made adjustments defensively way back when Jacques Demers was coaching. To me that's a great sign of character. At the same time, you look at that Detroit team with Kirk Maltby and Chris Draper—those types are typical character guys who bring it every night. Character can be shown in many different ways and in many different people.

You sound like a bit of a Detroit fan here.

I'm a big fan of Yzerman.

How did you get yourself out of a slump?

I can tell you, in my last year I hit every post, and I think I must have had six goals called back for some reason. I was the type of player who passed on a breakaway. I was always looking to make a play. I was not much of a shooter. It sounds kind of funny, but it didn't change my game. Obviously you want to score, but I got a lot of assists creating chances. I guess I didn't really dwell on that part of it. I didn't score as many goals as I would have liked to at the 2006 Olympics, but my first shot went right off the post and the second one hit the crossbar. It just wasn't meant to be. But I still obviously contributed, and again it goes back to your job with the team. If you allow slumps to hinder what you're doing on the ice on a daily basis it brings you down, and that's really detrimental. It's not easy to do, but you've got to just keep plugging away.

Describe some of the setbacks you've experienced and how you rebounded.

One of my biggest setbacks occurred in April 2004 when I took an awkward hit in our championship game. I knew something had happened right away, but of course, like any player, I just finished the rest of the game. It was the last game of the season, and I found out much later that I had bruised my spinal cord and my neck. All summer I rehabbed and then found out in September that I had rehabbed the wrong thing.

I got injured right away in practice and missed the first half of the season in 2005. When the doctor said, "You've bruised your spinal cord," I thought, as a female player who doesn't make a lot of money, maybe I should move on and do something else with my life. So for the first two weeks it was sort of retirement for me, and then I researched all the things I could do to get my neck strong and healthy and be able to take the physicality of hockey again. I hired a personal trainer, and just got away from the team and did what I needed to do for me. It was a very difficult thing to do. I was never the type not to train with the team; I always thought it was so important that everyone did things together. For that year I had to be selfish and say, "Listen, Cassie, you've got to take care of yourself right now; otherwise you're not going to mean anything to the team."

When I came back, I had essentially five or six key games to play to prove to the national team that I could still perform after the injury. I was under a bit of pressure because the coaches came to me and said, "If you're still injured we can't have you." I remember performing really well and scoring and getting points, but I also remember being able to take the physicality of the game. Three or four of those games were against the US. That was the biggest setback I have ever had to overcome in my hockey career. It was a pretty serious injury and came at a point in my career where I could have retired and been okay with it, but I'm glad that I pushed through it.

Do you have a story of some adversity that happened back in minor hockey or an earlier stage in your career that you grew from that might be of benefit to kids?

We were usually, as elite players, among the best in our age group. I remember hearing things from other teams and parents like, "She thinks she is so good." I'm a pretty sensitive person, I like to be around people, and I'm a people-pleaser type of person, but I developed hard skin during those times. I remember having a coach at university who blamed me any time we lost or tied, even when my mom came to the game. It was such a terrible year, and I almost quit hockey because of it.

I think I developed a little thicker skin at a younger age, especially with only three or four of us really being high-profile in the female game. I knew about jealousy and all those things, but I believe that I did things the right way and for the right reasons, and that's all you can do. Just let the negative stuff that goes on behind you slide off. It's easier to do if you believe you're doing what's right for the game, you're nice to people, and you have good values and morals. You're going to make mistakes and you're going to have to admit that, but you can't allow people who are just jealous to bring you down; you really can't. Wayne Gretzky had to deal with that, and I'm sure it's a more prevalent problem for boys in minor hockey because that's such a competitive world. But it's a fact of life, and you either learn to deal with it or you don't.

So don't allow a coach who treats you poorly or puts you down, or anyone else, reduce your ability to follow your dream?

Yeah, I think so. Obviously I would never encourage anyone to step all over people to follow their dream, but we were told girls and women shouldn't play hockey. Even my dad was like, "You should be a tennis player or a golfer. You'd make more money playing tennis." He just thought of it as an economic thing. As girls we were told constantly that we shouldn't play, and had I listened I would have quit like a lot of my girlfriends did at 16 or 17. Where would I be now? I wouldn't have had the chance to go to the Olympics. There will always be a lot of naysayers no matter what you do, but you have to believe in what you're doing. If it's a good environment for you, just go for it.

How did you handle pressure?

I loved it. I welcomed it. This is a bit outside of hockey, but I took a job after the 2002 Olympics with the NHL network. It was cable television, and there weren't a lot of people watching, but for me being the only female, I thrived on wanting to be a good role model. I wanted to know my stuff and to prove that I was there because I knew my stuff, not because I was female. That was a pressure situation, but I just combatted it with hard work and by being as prepared as I could be. People who don't handle pressure very well are people who aren't prepared. From our team perspective, after winning gold in 2000 and the pressure of winning again in 2006, if we had lost it wouldn't have been due to lack of preparation. It would have been something out there that we just weren't supposed to win.

What are the qualities of a closely knit team, and how do you create team chemistry?

Knowing each other is huge, because not everyone wants to be around the team all the time. For me, team time was when I needed to be at practice and at the game. Other than that, I would have preferred to just sit at home and read a book rather than go out with the girls for dinner. So I think understanding what makes each team member click and being professional about it is important. A good example of that kind of understanding is when we went to Valle Peligna a week prior to going to the Olympic village in 2006. Everyone was so crusty, and we were so tired. We had people who were sick, we had just come off a tough training block, and this was supposed to be our week of rest. As a team, we had rules. We weren't allowed to wear jeans in a public setting like a team function. We were never allowed to drink, obviously, during competition. I felt it was so important for us as a team, without the coaching staff, to go to a nice restaurant and wear jeans and have a glass of wine and just sort of release a layer of crust that we women can never hide. As a leadership group we knew this was the best thing for our team because of who they were. We knew they couldn't sit in their hotel room another night. I don't think you learn those things about each other without team building.

We held a three-week camp on Prince Edward Island in the summer of 2005. There were three to a cottage: an older player, a middle-aged player, and a young player. We had to get to know each other and learn to work well together. As part of the team building we set it up so one night a certain cottage cooked for another cottage and vice versa. On top of the boot-camp regimen, we did a lot of team-building activities and I think we really got to know each other and therefore the camp was better than other years. It showed on the ice how well we worked together.

Pat Quinn says that trust is the glue; that's his favourite word. What do you see in trust, and how did you build trust as a captain?

Trust is key, for sure. I think trust amongst teammates is more important than trust in the coach, per se. If you trust each other as teammates you can go in a direction that the coach may not take you, with or without trust. The players who are going behind teammates' backs and talking to the coach really become less a part of the team. Automatically you say, "Well I don't trust that person or what they're saying to the coach," and so they become blackballed or pushed to the side. I saw that a lot over my career. I thought about how to build trust by having my actions represent what I was saying, going to bat for my teammates and getting the leadership group on the same page. It is crucial that the girls trust the leadership group, and agree not to disagree in public. We could disagree behind closed doors, but not in front of everyone else. This was a leadership group and we had to be together on issues and not talking about each other behind backs. So I think you build trust by just walking the walk. People trust you if what you're saying and what you're doing are the same things.

Not everybody's going to get along in life. Does everyone have to get along to function on a team?

I don't think so. There definitely has to be a level of professionalism. There were relationships on our team that were on-ice only. Some of the women were not going to talk much outside of the rink, but at the rink they were professionals and you didn't notice anything on the ice. As long as that's happening then no, I don't think everyone has to get along.

What is your best description of a team player?

A team player is someone with integrity, someone who is real, someone who admits his or her mistakes, who has a great work ethic, who has passion, who really buys in to what's going on, and who admits when they have bad days, someone who shows up every day and brings the best that she or he can to the table. In the NHL, I think sometimes leaders are picked because of their offensive capabilities and what the club wants them to be in the community. That's how you're seeing leaders picked more and more nowadays, but I think they should be people who are there for the right reasons, 110 percent of the time, for the team. It doesn't necessarily have to be the best player. If it is, great, but it doesn't have to be the best player.

Have you ever had to put aside personal values to fit in as part of the team?

No, I don't think so. Maybe I'm lying to you because sometimes I maybe tried to act younger when I was with the young kids. I tried to be, "Hey, I'm cool like you," so I would go with the girls who are shoppers to the funky shoe stores. I would go to those places with them and try to hang out with them, but I don't think I changed who I was. I tried to make myself normal to them and didn't put myself on a pedestal. As far as changing values and morals, I think the worst thing captains can do is change who they are and where they come from and what they're about.

As a young player, who was your idol?

I was a defenceman and a forward pretty much most of my career; I always switched back and forth. I loved Paul Coffey. I loved to watch him skate, and I tried to emulate him when I played defence. As a forward, I wanted to be like Steve Yzerman. I didn't have his goal-scoring capability, but I definitely had the offensive prowess, and I could play a two-way game. One day Yzerman was on the first line, next he was sort of the third-line guy, and he was still contributing. You didn't ever see him pouting with all the injuries he'd been through. I really like someone like that. We didn't have female players to look up to when I was growing up, so my role model was my mom, my parents. I watched my dad go to work every day at six in the morning and come home at seven at night, and my mom just worked so hard in everything she did. Because there were no females in the NHL, for the most part my brothers, sisters, and parents were definitely my role models.

Do you have any other specific memorable minor hockey experiences?

One of my fondest memories was the Peterborough tournament, staying at the Holiday Inn. They had a pool where you could swim underneath [a wall] and then be outside. I'll never forget the Peterborough tournament. We used to go to it every single year and it was always between us and Peterborough and Brockville. We had such great teams back then. That was the best for me.

How did you handle school and sports? Was that ever an issue?

For a female athlete, school always has to come first and that's the bottom line. We don't have those big contracts to look forward to, so all the girls pretty much have an education of some sort. That was something you just did. It was a priority; it was priority number one, to be honest with you. Even now I don't know quite what I'm going to do, but I am thinking maybe I'll get my master's in business. School is important to me, so when I see some of the young athletes coming up that have sort of forgotten about school, it scares me a little bit. We really don't have a lot to fall back on if we don't have an education.

Your parents obviously had an effect on your minor hockey journey (your dad wanted you to be a tennis player). Did they help guide your direction early on or not?

My mom was always very athletic. She played softball. I remember going to watch her. She played professional football in 1969 in a three-team league, so she was a great role model as far as having an active and healthy lifestyle. My dad was a very practical man: "Well, not many girls play hockey, so why are you playing hockey? I know you're athletic, so why not play a sport where you have a chance to make money?" That's the way he thought. I was fortunate enough that both my parents supported me in whatever I was going to do. In my house, as long as I was doing well in school and in my extracurricular activities, the rules were flexible, but if those things slipped the clamp came down. So they were both very supportive in everything I did and, I think, honest with me, too. I appreciated their different techniques of parenting.

Who do you admire most, living or dead, and why?

I would have to say my mom, for sure. The things she's been through! My parents divorced when I was a young kid and continued to live in the same city. Both were very supportive, but I think essentially she raised us as a single mom. I've seen her start her own business and make a lot of money and lose that business and start another one. I admire how she's overcome the adversity that she's faced in her life. She is definitely a great role model, and she keeps fighting, and really, that's all you can ask for.

If you could choose somebody to be your neighbour, let's say somebody famous, who would it be and why?

Without question, Oprah Winfrey. I think she's obviously somebody who made a lot of money and has a great show, but she gives so much back to the world. A lot of people think that's not necessarily what you're supposed to do as a famous person who makes a lot of money, but I think it is. All of us who are in the public eye to some degree need to be giving back, and we need to make a difference because we have that ability. Oprah's someone who I think has gone above and beyond. She walks the walk. What she's done for the world is tremendous. She's someone who has been through a lot of adversity in her life, and look where she is.

If you hadn't played hockey, what might your future have been?

I think I would have been a teacher. If I hadn't played hockey, I think I'd be a grade 7 or Grade 8 teacher. This goes back to Miss Tibeiro and Miss Stapleton, my grades 7 and 8 teachers, who I loved and who I believe had a great impact on my life. Those are the years, I think, in which a teacher can make or break a kid and help them and guide them. Now, I really would like to continue broadcasting, but I think had I not had all those opportunities, I'd still pick teaching.

Scott Niedermayer

Scott Niedermayer has nearly run out of fingers to display his championship rings. He has won the World Junior Championships, an Olympic gold medal in 2002 at Salt Lake City, the World Cup, the World Championships, the Memorial Cup, and four Stanley Cups. Born in Edmonton, Alberta, Scott lived his minor hockey years in Cranbrook, BC. In 1991, as a Kamloops Blazer, he was named the CHL Scholastic Player of the Year and a member of the WHL First All-Star Team, an accolade he repeated again one year later. He won the Memorial Cup, was named to the Memorial Cup All-Star Team and was the tournament's MVP, as well, in 1992.

The New Jersey Devils chose Niedermayer as their first-round (third overall) pick in 1991. He recorded one assist in his first four games as the youngest player to ever play for the Devils before returning to junior. In 1992–93, his first of 12 straight seasons with New Jersey, Niedermayer was named to the NHL All-Rookie Team and the following year helped New Jersey achieve its first-ever 100-point season. In 1996–97 Niedermayer amassed a team-leading 18 power play points while simultaneously helping the Devils achieve the best defensive record in the league and the 104 points that won them the Eastern Conference and Atlantic Division regular season titles. The following season of 1997–98 was like an instant replay when the Devils again allowed the fewest goals in the league, won both the Eastern Conference and Atlantic Division season titles, and set new franchise records for most wins (48) and most points (107) in a season.

Niedermayer played in the NHL All-Star Game in 1998, 2001, and 2004 and was selected again, though he was unable to play, in 2007. He was also named to the NHL First All-Star Team in 1998, 2004, and 2007. He won an astonishing three Stanley Cups with the Devils in 1995, 2000, and 2003, as well as the James Norris Trophy for Defenceman of the Year in 2004, when he scored a career high of 54 points.

In 2005 Anaheim signed Niedermayer as a free agent, enabling him to play with his younger brother, Rob. In his first season with the Ducks, Niedermayer tallied his best-ever regular season point total, while the team advanced to the Western Conference Finals. Scott represented Canada for a second time in the 2006 Winter Olympics and in December won the Mark Messier Leadership Award for his leadership skills on and off the ice. He finished the season by setting yet another personal record for most points alongside a slew of franchise records, including most points in a season, most wins in a season, and best overall record culminating in the Anaheim Ducks' first Stanley Cup victory. Scott, again named to the NHL's First All-Star Team, was also fittingly awarded the coveted Conn Smythe Trophy as the Most Valuable Player of the Stanley Cup Playoffs.

Niedermayer welcomed his third Stanley Cup home to Cranbrook in September 2003, not only to his wife Lisa and their sons Logan, Jackson, and Joshua, but to the whole community as well. He invited the public for an autograph and photo with the Cup at the home arena of the Kootenay Ice, took the Cup on a train trip through Fort Steele, and brought it out to 400 firefighters battling the forest fires that had forced 175 families from their homes. It must have been much easier on brother Rob, and possibly more satisfying to Scott, when his fourth Stanley Cup arrived in the summer of 2007, because this time it belonged to both of them.

The Interview

Who were the best leaders that you ever played with?

I played the bulk of my career with Scott Stevens and obviously know him well. He was the captain for about 11 years in New Jersey. I think leadership can take different forms. His strength as a leader was his work ethic, the way he would compete every night. I guess his style of leadership would fall under leading by example. He was in the league a long time and played a lot of hockey, and every practice and every game, for the most part, he was the hardest working guy, the guy with the most blocked shots, taking the body, and doing the difficult things. When you're a young player or a guy sitting on the bench and you see the captain doing those particular things, really, there's nothing that needs to be said at that point. It's all laid out in front of you. I was very fortunate to have been a teammate of his for as long as I was.

Do you emulate some of those qualities as a leader now?

I try to. I've probably learned a lot from him as far as how to take the leadership role and things that you have to do when you are in that position. I learned that if there's a practice or game, you go out there and play as hard as you can to help your team. If you have that attitude you're definitely going to give your team the best chance. It is important to build a strong team concept and a team identity that pays off down the way. It might not pay off that night, but if you keep the same attitude day in and day out, over the long haul I think your team is going to be headed in the right direction.

What qualities does a leader need?

I don't know if I'm overly confident as a leader at the moment. I'm pretty new to being a captain. I guess you get put in that position gradually. I was an assistant captain in New Jersey for a bit. As you get older, you take more of a leadership role and then all of a sudden you get the "C" on your jersey and that's sort of like, here you go, let's see what you can do. I guess I've been with teams that have done very well, and I've been around enough that now I realize what it takes to have success with a hockey team. I try to direct individuals and the team toward success by playing for the team, being willing to do the difficult things, and being willing to work hard even when I don't feel like it. I think all those little things essentially add up to everybody believing in and having confidence in each other and having confidence in the team as a unit. That obviously enables you to be at your best as a team.

Is leadership within the room more important today than ever?

It's hard for me to judge that. Though I think it's important, there are distractions. Everybody wants to do well personally and meet their own personal goals. You have to realize that everybody is out for themselves. I believe that's fair, but at the same time there's only so much playing time. It's not the easiest thing in the world to get that mindset of hard work and committing to the team. It is difficult because of the distractions that do pop up. I guess contracts and playing time all get mixed in there, and it's a matter of trying to say that if you buy into the team concept of helping each other out, eventually everybody's going to look good and benefit from having a team that does well. If you have some success as a team, usually everybody looks pretty good. When the team isn't doing well, one or two guys might look good because they have a few goals, but it's difficult to look good in general when your team isn't doing well.

How important are glue guys, and can you point to a couple that aren't in a leadership position, since not everyone can wear an "A" or a "C", but still help solidify leadership in the dressing room?

It's definitely important to have a bunch of guys that have been through it. One guy isn't able to just take control of the other 22 guys and be a leader for all of them, because some players have different responsibilities and respond differently. When you're able to have a handful of guys that are doing their job (and maybe they do it in different ways), and know what it takes to win and to have success, a lot of guys will respond to that. Some guys are going to be a bit more vocal and some guys respond to that. A player like Stevens does it by leading by example. The key is having different players with different leadership styles that hopefully cover the bases of your whole team and get the team playing together and going in the same direction.

What do you respect about the coaches you have played for?

After however many years I've played now, coaching has gotten to be one of the most difficult jobs. It's not easy. I talked about some of the distractions—you can't please everybody, and there is only so much ice time on a power play or even strength for forwards and defencemen. So, it's difficult. I respect, in a lot of ways, the commitment that these coaches have and the amount of time and effort they put into trying to help the team be the best it can be. I'm sure it's also mentally and emotionally tough. Nobody likes to be butting heads all the time with players so it's a difficult job. But, again, if a coach is strong and believes in what he's doing and obviously has been there and has knowledge, he can be very important in a team having success. There's no question.

How did coaches get the best out of you over the years?

It's definitely easier having different types of leaders and groups of guys on your team, as opposed to having one coach. I guess he has his assistants, but a lot of times the assistants will take on a slightly different role. It is difficult for a coach to lead in different ways with different players, so I think in a lot of ways it's up to the players to realize what message the coach is sending. That's what I've learned in my time. No matter how he's sending it, it's our job to get the message and not necessarily respond emotionally to how he's doing it.

What qualities do you respond best to in a coach?

I think I've changed in what I respond to as I've gotten older and more mature and have been around a bit in the game of hockey. Early in my career, my first coach, if I remember correctly, was Herb Brooks, and he wasn't really hard on me. I was a young player at the time. I was 19 and in a lot of ways he was encouraging and positive. I'm sure at the time I felt that was great. No one likes to be yelled at or made to sit on the bench. Then the following year Jacques Lemaire came in and he was more demanding of me and made me pay a price if I wasn't doing what he was trying to get the team to do as far as playing style. He wasn't overly vocal, he wouldn't do a lot of screaming and yelling, but if something wasn't right you weren't playing. It was difficult at the time, there's no question. I remember being very frustrated and wondering if that was the best way to go about it, but now, from where I'm sitting, having a bit of that tough treatment at the time was maybe the best way to get a message across. I think now I try to respond to any style of coaching by realizing that the coaches are trying to get their message across and that's the bottom line, but it's easier said than done sometimes.

In your estimation is motivation a coach's job, or in today's game is it more up to the player's initiative?

I think a coach can help, but obviously it has to come from each player if you're really going to have a team that is committed to winning and has what it takes to go through a playoff series and be there at the end of a playoff run. I don't think a coach can put that into a player; I think it has to be there. The coach can try and bring it out and do different things to help the players, but the players have to want it and be willing to sacrifice and willing to go through the grind that is a playoff run. I think the coach definitely is a part of it, but I think each player motivates himself and his teammates in a bigger way.

What are some of the things that coaches have done just to motivate and inspire?

It's the simplest of things. I've seen a lot of positive videos where the video coach shows a bunch of nice goals scored by the team and big hits and good plays and a couple of songs that get your blood flowing. When you leave the room after seeing something like that, you're excited and you have some confidence. I think that's a way to motivate players to want to go out and play and work together. On the flip side, there's the screaming and yelling. I don't know exactly how to put it in one word, the screaming's not necessarily to scare players, but to challenge players, to say, "You guys aren't doing what I think you can do and I'm not happy with that." In reality, I think both approaches are needed as opposed to just using one method all the time. I think it is probably the most effective when coaches can change it up like that.

You've been fortunate to be in a winning environment through a large part of your career. What is a winning environment, and how do you know when you're in one?

I have been lucky to have been part of some teams that have won championships, and really there is nothing better than doing that as a group of players. I think at the end of the day there's a feeling that when you hit the ice you know that each and every guy that you're going out there with is going to do his absolute best to help the team win. It's a lot of work to create that feeling. You can't just sort of snap your fingers, but once you have it, obviously you have to stay on top of it. You can't take a night off because it's difficult to get it back. It's a feeling that you're just going to do your absolute best on the ice and because of that you have confidence and you'll have success. It's tough to do in all 82 games.

There are probably not many teams that have done it for 82 games. There's always a little bit of a letdown stretch where you think you can put the feet up a bit and coast, but that never works really. Over five or six games it will catch up to you.

How do general managers and coaches affect that winning environment?

I think the general manager needs to find the right type of player that is willing to commit that much and give that much to the team because I don't think necessarily everybody is. Maybe you don't need 22 guys totally dedicated that much, but you need the bulk of your team to be that dedicated to helping the team have success. Obviously the general manager is in charge of the personnel on the team and who's in the dressing room and who isn't. I think that is very important.

With the coaching staff, a lot of the questions that you've asked so far about what can they do to motivate players, build confidence, establish strategy, and how a team plays—that is their role in having that success. They are both very important roles. In professional hockey you can take it a step further. It is also important that the ownership is confident and stable and gives resources to the general manager and has confidence in the general manager and gives him the time to work out his plan, because it's difficult to change directions every year or two and build that winning atmosphere.

One thing that hit me when you talked about having people who are in the mode of paying the price is, at the end of the day, you're talking about players who are hungry.

I think you can be hungry for different things. There are plenty of guys who are hungry. It's not so much a thought as just a feeling. I guess it starts as a thought, but it's more than that. It's a feeling in your gut that you're going to go out there and be willing to do as much as you possibly can, whether it's scoring a big goal or doing a bunch of little things that are as important in a long playoff run like blocking shots, you're just willing to do it. You're willing to go through whatever may be in front of you. You have it in your gut that that's what you're going to do. I'm sure hunger can be learned, I'm sure it can be taught to some degree, but I think at the same time there are some people who have that hunger naturally.

So on that theme, what motivates or drives you?

I think now that I've had success, it's just realizing how special that is and wanting to do it again. To sit back after two long months of playoff hockey and realize that you're the last team standing, and everybody's had a big part in it and you've done your part, is pretty satisfying. I mean, anytime you have a goal and you do all you can and do your best at it, it's a satisfying feeling, and I guess that's the motivation now.

What would the keys be to your preparation for a game?

Obviously for the big games I don't have a problem with the motivation. I have no problem with getting excited. I think the biggest thing for me is to try and just stay focused and not think about anything else: like what could happen if you do this or if you don't do that; if you win, this will happen; if you lose, that will happen. I'm at my best when I'm focused on what is right in front of my nose and not worrying about anything else. That allows me to put everything I have into playing hockey. If you're thinking about other things then you're not using everything you have for what's right in front of you. Just try to be focused and have a clear mind, and, like I said, the excitement and energy, the crowd, it's just there in big games so that's really a non-issue.

I'm hearing from a bunch of guys the terms "practice mindset" and "playing mindset." For you, what is the difference between these two mindsets?

It's definitely important to be prepared in practice and to go out and work hard and to practice at a high speed as you would in a game. Those things are definitely important, but in practice there's no opponent per se, there's no scoreboard for the most part, and you can work on things. You maybe can think a little bit more. Once you get into the game, you want to let what you practised, how you played over your career, and everything sort of just take over. In a game you want what you know to just come out.

How do you prepare in the months, weeks, and days leading up to a season?

It depends on when and how we finished. If we lost out early in the playoffs, and it's going to be a long summer, there's a lot more time to really get involved in a fitness program and work on areas that I want to work on. If we've gone to the finals and summer is going to be over in two months, I find I need to rest. I need to mentally and physically have time away from the demanding nature of sports and hockey. If we've gone to the finals in June, that doesn't leave me with a whole lot of time to work on the fitness side of it. I still obviously try to stay in good shape and be ready for camp, but I might not have as much time to work on weaknesses as I would have if I had the four months off. I feel it's more important to be fresh physically and mentally going into camp than maybe being in my total best physical condition after a short summer.

Another thing that I've learned has been good for me, and I think a lot of players are starting to do it more, is finding time during the season to work out and keep my strength up. I found early in my career that I would put all this energy into the summer training and come to camp in great shape and strong and the whole thing, but if I had some testing done at about game 40, I'd notice my strength levels had dropped. You want to maintain a high level of fitness right through the season and, more importantly, be ready for the playoffs. A lot of players are taking fitness maintenance a lot more seriously now, including me. I find it works trying to sneak these workouts in during the season once in a while. You might be a little stiff for a game, but I think that's a small price to pay for being a stronger player down the road and in better condition than you would be if you didn't do it during the season.

How do you develop mental toughness and approach the mental side of the game?

I think that the mental side of the game, in many ways, is a game in itself. I mean, obviously you need some physical abilities, but if your mental strength isn't there it doesn't matter how fast you can skate or how hard you can shoot the puck, you're probably not going to have the success that you want. The mental part is a big part of the game, and one you're always learning about. We spoke earlier about how a coach treated me when I was younger and maybe then I wasn't really mentally ready to handle some of the tougher situations. Now I've been through it and I found that I'll be around to play another game even if I was sitting on the bench for the last half. I'm more capable of handling that kind of situation mentally in addition to the ups and downs that are going to happen during the season and during a game. You're going to go out one shift and maybe make a mistake. The trick is the next play: don't let it happen again. Do your best and don't dwell on it. There are a lot of important things that need to be learned mentally to compete in any sport, including hockey, for sure.

What is confidence to you and why is it hard to identify for most people?

I think it takes a lot to build confidence. You can't just say, "I want to have confidence," and instantly have it. It's hard work first, and you have to have dedication. Eventually things start to pay off for you, and you start to have a bit of success. Once you have that success you can't just say, "Well now I have it." It's something you have to keep working on all of the time. I know personally there are certain times during a year where I feel that things are working really well and I believe in everything I'm doing out there. Then there are going to be other stretches where there are questions in the back of my head, and I'm not quite as sure of myself. I think that's always going on. There's probably no player that has full confidence all the time. You have to realize when you don't have it and find ways to get it back.

Do you use self talk to stay confident?

I think that's important. I don't think anybody's positive all the time, but it helps that the more positive thoughts you have in your head, the more positive things you say. Then if you go out and try to do what you say, the better off you're going to be and the better chance you've given yourself to gain confidence. You're really sort of slowing yourself down with the more negative things you think and there's no question that you're making it tougher on yourself to get back to where you want to be.

Talk to us about some of your most exciting moments as an athlete.

Probably my most exciting was the first Stanley Cup we won in 1995 with New Jersey. I was 21, so I was young, and at that point you are playing with a lot of excitement and emotion. We talked about how I wasn't quite as mentally mature maybe as I am now, 11 years later. I've learned a lot since then, but there's no question that when we were one game away from winning my first Stanley Cup it was a dream come true for every player. I don't think there's any question that that first time winning the Stanley Cup was when I was the most excited.

How important is character to being a high-performance player?

I think it's very important. In my mind, character is a combination of the mental approach to the game and the hunger to win that you were talking about. I think those two things help make up your character. Character is how you are as a person, the choices you make, and how you treat other people. When you get on the ice, your character determines how hard you are willing to compete for your teammates and your team and yourself. I believe those are the qualities that make up most people's character.

I'm going to ask you about a slump. Describe a time when you weren't producing and tell us how you broke out of it.

There have been plenty of those. The trick is to know the best way to get out of it. As difficult as it may seem, you have to be positive; you have to realize that you've done it before and you will do it again. It's just a matter of getting through the stretch as quickly as you can. It's continuing to work hard, continuing to do all the little things where you can add value as a player. Maybe you feel like you're having a slump and you're not getting the points or not scoring the goals that you feel you should. It's important at a time like this to just go out there and be effective and help the team. There's a lot of value in that. I think you need to learn to appreciate that as player, you're going out there and helping your team. You might not be scoring the goals at that moment, but you're doing other things that are helping your team succeed. To help myself feel positive, if I feel that the puck isn't finding the net for me, I'll get a video of a few of the goals that I've scored in the past and stick it in for five minutes and just watch it again. It helps to actually see it on a TV screen that it can happen and it does happen. You have to be positive and have that belief.

Were there difficult situations you had to deal with as a player in minor hockey or junior hockey?

I'm not the best storyteller or the best at remembering things, but there were times when things weren't going as well as I would have liked. The one situation I can remember was when I was 18 and sent back to junior after spending a couple of months at the beginning of the season in New Jersey. I played a few games and was sent back in late November. At the time for me, and I think for most players, it was a big challenge going from the NHL back to junior, to a lower level, and then still having the commitment and just staying positive and being willing to continue to work hard when it felt like I'd sort of taken a step down. I felt I deserved to be somewhere else. It was tough, very tough, and I can't remember exactly how it went until the playoffs, but we ended up somehow figuring it out, because we had a playoff run and ended up winning the Memorial Cup that year. I know most of the regular season was difficult, but once playoffs rolled around it just became easier realizing there were goals right in front of me to take care of. That helped me to get things back on track.

What did you do to make that adjustment happen when you changed teams?

It was a new experience for me when I went to Anaheim. I'd been in New Jersey a long time and it was totally new for me to walk into a dressing room where I knew a couple of guys and that was about it. I didn't know where the tape was. I basically just kept my eyes and ears open and learned as much as I could about the players, about the staff, and just how things worked. I wanted to learn as quickly as I could and try to fit in as best I could right off the bat. Once you've got a grasp of your surroundings it is easier. I was an older player who had been given a leadership role on the team, so I wanted to figure out how I could help and what I could and couldn't do with the different players. Initially it's more of a quick learning process.

How do you personally handle pressure?

It's changed, I think, now that I'm older and I've had success, especially because I've had success in big games. There's less pressure on me now, and I think that helps me. It's not because I have any more skills or knowledge about how to deal with pressure, it's just because I've been there and I've done it. Experience takes away that feeling you get when it first happens. Now I know I've been there. I know that it will work out if I stick with the game plan. Like I said before, in preparing for big games, I think the best way to deal with pressure is to try and stay focused and have a clear mind. When you get into those big games there's no question there's pressure. You realize what can happen if you win the game or win the series. You know what it means, and it can be distracting, but you just have to say to yourself before you go to the rink, "Just try to clear your mind." Whether it's taking a little 15-minute walk or sitting and listening to music, if there are some thoughts in your head, let them run around for a bit and then try to get rid of them. Be ready to go when you get to the rink and stay focused on hockey.

How important is perseverance to an NHL career?

There are always ups and downs. Anybody who has been through it knows that's the nature of the game. You're going to play 82 games plus playoffs. You're going to have good ones; you're going to have bad ones. You're going to have a stretch where you feel confident in what you're doing out there. Then there are going to be stretches like you talked about when you're in a slump and things aren't going your way, and I think those are the times where perseverance obviously comes into play. These are times where you need to stick with the things that are no-brainers, such as the hard work, adding value to your team, blocking shots, hitting, just making good decisions with the puck, not turning it over, all those things that can help your team have success. Realize those things are never going to change and you need to keep doing them even if things aren't going your way or the team's way. Stick with those things through thick or thin. Perseverance is definitely needed in those difficult situations because if you give up you're not giving yourself a chance at all. When you stick with those things and persevere through them, you are giving yourself the quickest chance to turn it around.

What are the qualities of a closely knit team?

Really, at the end of the day, I've been on teams where there have been certain players who I wasn't the best of friends with. I probably disagreed with them on certain things, but when you get on the ice and have the same goal and the same commitment to that goal, I think that chemistry develops. Obviously you need to have players that get along well and have fun together. That's a big part of it, because when you're together as much as you are during a playoff run or a regular season, that's a lot of hours together on the plane and on the bus and in the dressing room. You need to get along, there's no question about it, but I think the basis for good chemistry is for everybody to be committed to the same goal. I think when that happens you're going to make things work.

How do teams build and maintain trust?

I think that takes time. You need to show your teammates that you will do the things your team needs you to do to succeed every game. It doesn't mean that you do it for one or two games in a row and take a break. You have to show that you're going to be doing those things every game and every shift, as best you can, and over a period of time you start to build that feeling and trust each other. Once that happens, then you get closer to that feeling that when you go out there you don't have to worry about anybody else on your team. You can just focus on your game and you know that the rest of the guys are going to be doing exactly the same thing. When you have that, it's a pretty good feeling, especially when you go out to play and feel that you can win the game no matter who you're playing.

What if players don't get along? Can a team still function at a high level?

I think it can, but you can't have too much friction because it can become a distraction. We've had teams that have had success while there have been disagreements between players. They don't hang out for dinner the night before a game and things like that. But obviously it can't be prevalent. There can't be little fights all over the place. If there are a couple of guys who don't get along but they get along with other guys on the team and everybody is committed to doing the best they can to help the team, I think that can be overcome. I don't think it's necessary for absolutely everybody to get along. If everyone is professional, disagreements can be overcome.

Describe a great team player for us.

A great team player is somebody who's committed to the team and doing what they can, what their strengths allow them to do, to help the team win. Whether that's going out and scoring goals and being the offensive threat that team needs, or being the guy who goes out and kills penalties, or maybe it's being the guy who gets out there two times a period and goes out and works as hard as he can, gets in a couple of hits, and then the rest of the time is supportive of the guys. There are so many different ways that players can be valuable to a team. Being a team player is doing whatever you can to help the team have success, on or off the ice.

How important is synergy to a team?

I think that comes about once the rest of the things are put together. Synergy is part of having that feeling of hitting the ice and just believing in each other, having trust in each other, knowing that each guy is out there committed to the team. If you hit the sweet spot where all that has happened, and guys have confidence playing with each other, then you have synergy. They know that if we do this then we'll be able to be an offensive threat or that we are confident we can slow down the offensive line on the other team because we've done it before. You can't just make that happen, you have to worry about all the other things and sort of hope that at the end of the day that synergy pops out. It's a big part of playoff hockey. You do all you can to give yourself a chance to have perfect synergy, and sometimes it happens and sometimes it doesn't, for whatever reason. You should be thankful when it comes about, and hopefully it lasts long enough to get you through.

Have you ever had to put aside personal values to fit in as part of the team?

Not that I can remember. It's hard to say never. I've played a long time and it's tough to be that certain about things, but I think, for the most part, I've been able to go out there and compete as hard as I can and have been supportive of my teammates without giving up my own values. Hockey is a physical game, and there are times when you're doing things on the ice that you maybe wouldn't do away from it, so in that sense maybe there have been times where I've done things that I maybe wouldn't have been proud of off the ice. Hockey is definitely a physical and emotional game and those things happen, but as far as fitting into a team or the atmosphere in the dressing room, I don't think there's ever been a time where I had to change things or be different.

As a young player, who was your hockey idol?

I sort of skipped around. I was just getting into watching hockey when the Islanders won their four Stanley Cups in a row, and I jumped on that bandwagon early on. Then I started following the Oilers. Obviously I was very lucky to watch that team play for a long time as I grew up in western Canada. There were so many Oilers fans I found myself just needing to cheer for somebody else, so when the Islanders were playing the Oilers I was an Islanders fan, but I loved watching Paul Coffey. Especially being a defenceman, Paul Coffey was the type of player that I enjoyed trying to be like. It was a lot of fun watching him. When Mario Lemieux came into the league, he was just amazing as well. The things he did offensively made him exciting to watch. There's not so much one player who stands out for me, but a handful that I enjoyed watching, for sure.

Could you take us back to a memorable hockey moment from minor hockey?

I grew up in Cranbrook, British Columbia, and I have been very fortunate right from day one basically being surrounded by a bunch of good hockey players and good friends that I made growing up playing hockey. We also had a lot of great coaches through our days in minor hockey. That's very important for a young player, so I was lucky. We were fortunate to win two provincial championships, one in peewee and one in bantam. Those were highlights, but so were the road trips, a lot of the horsing around in the hotels, the wrestling we used to do, and just stuff like that. That's a great part of childhood, and in a lot of ways those memories might be the best.

Who influenced your on-ice development?

My parents were very supportive. They were on all the road trips. I never remember going on a road trip without one of them being there. My mom wasn't working, so she would take us down to the rink for the skating lessons. My dad often was the manager of our team and was there on the road trips whenever he could be. I also had a coach named Len Bokay, who coached probably 80 percent of my years in minor hockey. He was a very good coach and I learned a lot from him. Besides my parents, he would be the next most influential person in my development.

How did you handle school and sport, and how did teachers handle you as you were trying to do that?

My parents always emphasized the importance of school. I had it drilled into me at a young age. I was probably like any other kid, not always believing what my parents said, but at the same time I had heard about the importance of school often, and I think it slowly got into my skull. I went away to Kamloops to play junior hockey for grades 11 and 12, and the team emphasized school. We were given a tutor once a week to make sure that we understood the school work that we had missed while on road trips. Up until I was about 17, I guess, the NHL seemed a different world than where I was. It seemed like something you watched on TV. I mean, I wanted to play in the NHL, but I don't know if it seemed totally real. I just realized that school was important and the goal of being able to find employment after your high-school and college days was what helped me stay focused.

Who do you admire most, living or dead, and why?

There are some amazing and great people out there for sure. My oldest son is seven years old so I'm not a totally new parent, but I'm not an old hat at it. I guess the easiest people to tell you about are my parents and grandparents. Just realizing how big a job and how difficult a job parenting is at times, and, I mean, it's also the most rewarding thing in the world. Obviously they are a big part of my life. They would probably get first billing in that department, but there are other people who have done some great things in the world who I definitely admire.

If you had a chance to talk to somebody, who would it be and why?

People ask these questions every once in awhile, and I'm not great at answering them. Again, it's the same type of thing. There are so many interesting people. You name one person and then you think, "Gee, it would be neat to talk to them," so it's a difficult question. I guess an interesting person to talk to would be Jesus Christ, for many reasons. I'm sure it would be interesting to hear him speak. Things that we learn now about his life, a lot of time has passed and a lot of different translations are out there, but to actually hear him and see him first-hand would be quite an experience I'm sure.

If you could perform any other occupation outside of sport, what would it be and why?

I'm just thankful I can play hockey because I don't know what I'd be doing if I wasn't. My dad is a doctor, so I think in a certain sense I enjoyed math and I enjoyed science in school. I'm sure that would have taken me somewhere, whether it would have been into medicine or science, I'm not sure. I'm sort of a "fact" type of guy. I enjoy things black and white, so I probably would have gone down that road, or at least I would be in that ballpark.

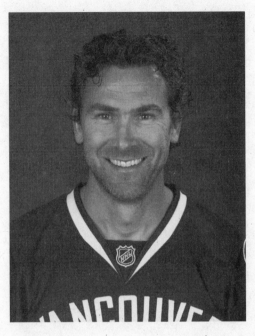

Trevor Linden

Born in Medicine Hat, Alberta, in 1970, Trevor Linden not only achieved his boyhood dream of playing junior hockey for the hometown Tigers, but also won two straight Memorial Cups with them. He was named to the WHL East Second All-Star Team and Memorial Cup Tournament All-Star Team in 1988 before becoming the Vancouver Canucks' first-round pick, second overall. At the conclusion of his inaugural season, the Canucks awarded Trevor with the Molson Cup, as well as the Most Exciting and Most Valuable Player awards after his 30 goals helped the Canucks make the playoffs for the first time in three years. He was selected to the NHL's All-Rookie Team, was a runner-up for the Calder Trophy, and was named Rookie of the Year by *The Hockey News*.

In 1991–92, Trevor became the Canucks' captain after playing as one of three co-captains the previous season. In addition, he played in his second consecutive All-Star Game and won his second Cyrus McLean Trophy for leading the team in scoring. In 1994 Trevor led his team to their first appearance in the Stanley Cup Final in 12 years and scored twice in game seven before losing a heartbreaker to the New York

Rangers. "Captain Canuck" held the NHL ironman record, playing in 482 consecutive games from October 4, 1990, to December 3, 1996, a Canucks record until it was broken by Brendan Morrison in 2007. He also compiled six seasons with 30 or more goals as a Vancouver Canuck.

Linden was traded to the New York Islanders on February 6, 1998, and was named captain less than one month later. Despite leading the Islanders with eight power-play goals the following season, Trevor was traded to the Montréal Canadiens on May 29, 1999. He scored 30 points and registered a 56.3 face-off percentage in just 50 games during his first season as a Hab. Trevor won his first NHL Player of the Week honour on October 23, 2000, scoring eight points in three games.

On March 13, 2001, Linden was traded to the Washington Capitals before being traded back to the Canucks on November 10, 2001. He proceeded to succeed Stan Smyl as the all-time Vancouver Canuck points leader. He also leads the Canucks in all-time goals scored and most games played, and on October 5, 2006, he became the first Vancouver Canuck to score 300 goals.

Trevor Linden has been a member of Team Canada at the World Junior Hockey Championships, twice at the World Championships, the World Cup of Hockey, and the Olympics. He created the Trevor Linden Foundation in 1995, tirelessly supports Canuck Place, a hospice for terminally ill children, and was awarded the King Clancy Memorial Trophy in 1996–97 for his humanitarian community contributions. In 2003 Trevor received the Order of British Columbia.

An extremely hard-working president of the National Hockey League Players' Association (NHLPA) from 1998 to 2006, he has played more than 1,000 games in the NHL. The man of iron is also an avid bike racer who completed a 67-kilometre cross-country mountain bike race very appropriately named the "Squamish Test of Metal."

The Interview

Who were the best leaders you ever played with and what qualities made them that way?

The quieter, focused, lead-by-example leadership style works best for me. I was fortunate enough to play with Steve Yzerman in the Canada Cup tournament and the Olympics. Early in his career, Steve was criticized because he wasn't that vocal, grab-the-guy-by-the-scruff-of-the-neck and-tell-him-what-to-do kind of leader, but now he is revered as one of the great leaders because he's the quiet, professional, lead-by-example kind of guy.

The other thing I admire about Steve is the amount of respect he has for every player. I first met Steve in 1991 when I played my first All-Star Game. Actually, it was during the Gulf War. I was very shy. I didn't know anyone and certainly none of the top guys. I remember standing in the hallway before introductions to the All-Star Game in the Chicago Stadium that year. It was an amazing atmosphere, and Steve took the time to talk to me. I will never forget that. Steve respected the people around him whether it was the trainers or other players, and I think that says a lot about leadership.

When I talk about coaches who I thought were great leaders, as well as great coaches, the one guy who comes to mind is Pat Quinn. Pat was the master of respecting his players. He gave respect and got respect back. I believe that's a critical component of leadership, whether you are a manager, coach, or player.

You've worn a "C" and an "A" in your career. What are your strongest leadership qualities?

I look at myself not as the most talented or gifted player, but I have always considered myself someone who wanted to be dedicated, hard working, and lead by example. As I matured as a leader, I realized it's less of what you say and more of what you do. Leadership is how you carry yourself and how you react and act in all sorts of circumstances, whether that's after the game, before the game, or at dinner with the guys.

How important is leadership going to be in the "new" NHL? Will it be accentuated?

Even in the last couple of years I feel the game of hockey has become more than ever a sport where "teams" win. I'm a big sports fan. I like basketball, but hockey isn't like basketball, where you can have the best two players and win the game. In hockey you have to have a team of 20 guys committed to one common goal. Over the last few years that's been the major driving force behind successful teams, and that's leadership from within. The key to the success of a team is certainly to have a coach who can lead, but your leadership, your maturity level, and the quality of character in your room is what puts you over the top most times.

John Maxwell says that leadership is influence. How do you influence now without being the team's captain? What is your role?

This is interesting because when I was 22 or 23, I watched an older player come from a very successful team who'd won a Stanley Cup. I watched how he worked with young guys. His name was Ryan Walter. I'm being sincere and honest when I say that the biggest thing I learned from Ryan Walter was to almost approach it from a different angle, not from a leadership standpoint, but a "Hey you know what, I'm on your level. I want to befriend you and work with you" standpoint. So you're not coming from a sense of power, not coming from the position of "I'm above you, I have a 'C' on my jersey," but from an even playing field. What I really like now is that I'm not a guy on the power play anymore, I'm not one of the top guys on the score sheet, so I can come and almost identify the guys that need a tap, a pat on the back, or it may be grabbing that guy after practice and shooting some pucks. I see the game from a different standpoint now. I was very young in the early 1990s, and I watched you work with different players and saw how you dealt with the guys on the fourth line. You brought a sense of pride to what you were doing and sent it through our team. That was something that has always stuck with me. Now I'm kind of in that same boat and it has really paid dividends for me.

Coaching at the NHL level has transitioned; it's not an easy job. What do you respect about some of the coaches you've played for, not just from a leadership point of view but also from a coaching point of view?

No question, it's one of the most difficult jobs. Outside of what I said before, the respect factor, I think the best coaches have the ability to adjust, assess situations, and not get over-reactive. One of the things I admire most about Marc Crawford is his ability to digest what's happened either the period before or the night before. As intense and emotional as Marc can get, he's able to move forward very quickly. That's an excellent quality. The other thing is he is able to say, "We had a bad game last night but this is what we're going to do to fix it." As a player, that's what I want to know. I know we got our butts kicked the night before, but give me a plan so we can get better. That's the best message I can get from a coach, not what we did wrong after a game. I pretty much know. You can tell me again, and that's fine, but how are we going to fix it? That's what he's really good at.

We asked 12 NHL coaches for our book Simply the Best: Insights and Strategies from Great Hockey Coaches *how they got the best out of players. Now we want to ask players how did coaches get the best out of you? What scenarios did coaches create to make you the very best athlete?*

I think the key to being a coach is that you have to understand character and personalities and what works for different guys. It's not a one-size-fits-all situation. For me personally, a pat on the back goes a lot further than an earful. I don't need someone to give me an earful because I self-talk a lot, and I'll give myself an earful.

When I came back to Vancouver, I was petrified because I'd left here and come back after four years. The thing I really admire and will never forget, the best thing that Marc and Jack and Mike did was to give me a game plan. That enabled me to focus on exactly what I had to do, so I wasn't coming into a situation where I tried to do everything, tried to do it all. I was very focused. They brought me in and set my course, and when they saw me getting off it, they put me back on. That was a big key for me and really helped me in my transition.

How much of a coach's job is motivating the player? Does it come from the coach or is it demanded as part of the player's initiative?

I really believe that the motivation comes from believing in the game plan and having a game plan that makes sense. I believe less motivation is needed with the modern-day athlete and I think a key to motivation is structure. Guys grow up wanting to win, to be the best. Part of putting a team together is having guys who are like that, but I think a lot of coaching is setting the right environment for motivation. The old "win one for the Gipper" motivation is really a thing of the past.

Has there been a coach who really picked up on that, communicated to you on your level, and was better than others?

I've had the luxury (I don't know if it's a luxury or not) of playing for a lot of different coaches, but certainly I've always admired a coach who will speak to you one-on-one and take the time to call you in and say exactly what he wants so there's no miscommunication. I've always appreciated that. I've never been one to respond to getting called out. I think there are too many guys who resort to that, although there are times when it's necessary, in certain situations.

You talked about building an environment. How do general managers and coaches build a winning, successful environment?

It's one of the things I really was impressed with when I came to Vancouver. There was a plan here, a set plan, a framework, a blueprint of how they were going to win, and it wasn't on a game-to-game basis but a year-to-year basis. They probably had a three- to five-year plan in their minds. I think that is key because the players start to buy into that and over time it's like osmosis, the plan sinks in. I saw it with this group; it started to sink in and players started to believe. I'm not sure exactly how you do it, but I was part of it over the last three or four years, and it came from the staff here in Vancouver. I know from a player's standpoint that it takes a little bit, but then it starts to sink in and take hold. It's critical because without a plan on a game-to-game basis, you're kind of like a ship without a rudder. You're just kind of floating around out there, and hopefully the wind blows you one way or the other. But when you have a plan and you don't deviate, you do the best. If you get off course sometimes, you get back to your blueprint.

How do players affect that winning attitude or atmosphere?

Certainly it's by believing in what you're doing, and it's always helpful to have success. A little success goes a long way.

What motivates and drives you? You've been at this game for a long time. Did things motivate you when you were younger that don't now, or is it the same stuff?

When I played junior and when I was growing up, I always wanted to be a National Hockey League player. That was my goal, that was my dream, and I've always pushed myself to be as good as I can be. Like I said before, I don't think I've always been the most talented guy. I always tried to work as hard as I could and apply myself as well as I could. Today it's a little different, obviously, for me. What drives and motivates me now is to win the Stanley Cup. I look at people who have won and I literally picture myself holding the Cup. I watch every year when they hand the Cup out, and I have trouble thinking there's anything better than that.

How do you prepare for your best game?

I've always been a player who likes to play in important games. I get mad at myself because I play so poorly in pre-season, but I guess the bottom line is those games don't matter except for getting yourself some conditioning and getting your timing back. I have been fortunate to play for some coaches who have helped to simplify things. I try to talk to myself. It's like anything else. I try to establish a foundation for myself, think about what things are the foundations to my game, the three or four pillars that I can build my game on. I want to start with that early in the game and kind of build off it. Today those foundations are certainly different because I'm asked to do different things. On a team every player is asked to do different things, so I try to identify those and start doing some very simple things early.

You have been traded. How did you adjust to the new team, and how did you adjust to being traded?

Being traded was probably one of the hardest things that ever happened to me. The first time it was difficult, very difficult. I had never been traded in junior. I played in Medicine Hat for three years, and then I came to Vancouver and played 10 years here and really felt a bond to those two teams. I'm a guy who needs to feel a part of something. Once I was traded, it took me awhile to really feel comfortable. Some guys get traded and light it up right away, but for me it was kind of the opposite. I needed to get my feet anchored before I could feel that I was a part of things.

What were some of the more difficult situations you had to face as a young athlete, not only as a pro, but maybe in the "Hat" or minor hockey?

I was so competitive as a 12- or 13-year-old. But in hindsight, when you're 12 or 13 years old work as hard as you can but enjoy the game. I can't

think of any real hardships. I feel very fortunate to have parents who got me to the games and were very supportive.

How did you develop mental toughness?

It's a work in progress, as you mature and grow as a player and a person. I probably learned some from my mom, not that she was a big hockey gal, but she was someone who expected us to keep our composure. If we didn't, we would be missing a few games. I've learned things along the way, too, and even now I watch how our coaching staff asks for and defines mental toughness. It's difficult to define. It's almost something you need to teach players. I think it's taught more now, but when I started it was all about how you reacted to certain situations. What's the best way to react to certain situations, to lose your cool and start running around when you get scored on early? No. The right way to judge a situation is something that should be taught. It's taught more now than it was before, but I'm still learning from our coaching staff and certainly from different players, too.

Talk about that elusive word "confidence." Describe it in your terms. How do you get confidence? How do you lose it?

Confidence is something that is unfortunately confused with cockiness or being high on yourself. As a kid, when I heard someone described as being confident it wasn't a good thing. Looking back, I wish that I had been a bit more, I don't want to say cocky, that's not the right word, but there's nothing wrong with believing in what you're doing and believing in yourself in anything you do. If you're the type of player who constantly has to prove to himself night in and night out, it's a tough gig and it gets hard. Confidence grows when you are younger, and I think it almost has to be kind of nurtured along by parents. When things aren't going well for me, and my confidence is low and I don't feel good with the puck or things aren't going my way, I guess the easiest thing for me to do is just go back to square one, back to the foundation, just start over and find my confidence. That doesn't always work for me because I could look for a long time! I try to go back to the foundation and basically look at the principles of my game that can at least help the team be successful. Go back to square one and work back to where you are feeling good with the puck or feeling confident. It's an elusive thing.

What was your most exciting moment as an athlete?

For me it was probably team success, and that was probably beating Toronto in the conference final in 1994. I always say that because we won. Everybody asks, "What about the Stanley Cup final?" Well, it wasn't [my most exciting moment] because we lost. Beating Toronto, at home at the old Coliseum, was a thrill, and one of my most favourite moments.

How important is character to being a high-performance player?

I think it's critical. It goes back to the old foundation. You and I have seen tons of guys with skill and ability who didn't have the intangibles. Whether you want to call that character or not, it's what completes a player. Character is dedication. Being down to earth, respectful, those are keys that I find all the top players have. I have the most respect for Joe Sakic. He's an amazingly talented player, and he's got all those qualities. He's down to earth, he's thoughtful, he's hard-working, he's dedicated, and so is Jarome Iginla, or Paul Kariya. They are all quality, hard-working people, people you want to associate with.

Talk to us about setbacks or adversity and how you rebounded.

I think that this was an issue for me early in my career because I really analyzed a loss. I was guilty of taking a regular season loss too hard. There is a fine line between dwelling on failure and then having that hangover effect for a day or two, because it wears you out. I was always a responsible player, even as a kid, and I almost feel I carried some of that with me too long. We're talking in junior, after the game, you didn't talk on the bus, you didn't talk the next day, and I'm not sure that was the right way to go about it. I think it almost took me seeing a guy like Glen Hanlon come into the room after a tough playoff loss, with us being down in the series and facing elimination, and saying, "Hey, it takes four games to win; they haven't got four yet, have they?" for me to immediately click out of depression and move into, "What do we have to do to get out of this hole?" For me the transition was always pretty slow. I think that improves, but my biggest problem as a young player was dwelling either on a poor individual performance or a poor team performance, and that wasn't helpful to me being on top of my game all the time.

Have the principles you used to get over adversity in the game helped you with personal adversity?

I've had a huge personal growth period. I've come to the understanding that things happen in life for a reason, and it's about making sense of why and trying to learn from that and understanding what direction I'm supposed to go. It's helpful when you view any experience, good or bad, as something that is going to shape you. If you grow from it and become better from it, it's not such a bad experience. I thought getting traded in 1998 the first time was the worst thing that ever happened to me. In hindsight, it was probably the best thing that ever happened to me. It allowed me to realize how great Vancouver was.

Pressure's an issue for all of us. When have you felt the most pressure? How do you handle it?

I probably felt the most pressure when I went to Montreal. I was traded from Vancouver to New York and New York to Montreal, and boy, I tell you, I had been in the league 12 years, but at that point, I felt pressure. I thought long and hard about the best way to go about this and I think that I put too much pressure on myself. It's probably my character. It's a double-edged sword. Being responsible is good, but you can also load yourself up too much and it's like you've got a weight on your back. I look at big games and important playoff games and it's a different style of pressure, a pressure that I almost look forward to. When I go through situations like that, as nervous as I am during the day—and I'll never forget back here at home against St. Louis for game seven I was so concerned about myself—even before the game, the minute the puck drops I'm just on autopilot. I just know what to do.

How important has perseverance been to your career?

I think it's been a real lesson for me, because in Montreal there were nights where we were struggling. You're in a great city, it's a great hockey market, and things aren't going well, and it's almost like it's a battle to keep yourself positive and motivated. This was the same guy that came to Vancouver in the early 1990s and used to always say, "The sun came up today, isn't that great?" As tough as things may seem, when you lose that third game in a row, you've got to find the positive somewhere. That's a lesson in perseverance which requires a lot of character, something I continue to work at.

What was the toughest part for you in the whole collective bargaining Agreement negotiations?

I think trying to find the balance of the right thing to do. That was hard. I never had a problem; at least I didn't think I did, because it really wasn't about me. I had played 17 years in the league and I was 34 years old. It wasn't about me. The guys I really felt for were the guys in years three, four, or five, some on the bubble, some who had just made the National Hockey League. If I had never played another game in the league, I would still have been thrilled and felt fortunate for the time I spent in the NHL, but I felt for the guys who weren't in my situation. I think trying to balance off listening and talking to 700 different guys with different situations and trying to do the right thing was probably what weighed on my mind the most, and probably cost me several hours of sleep.

How do you get a closely knit team?

The biggest thing is respect. It's your top guys, the guys who are counted on every night to score, who are on the power play, who play 25 minutes a game, having the utmost respect for the guy who plays seven minutes and who gets spot shifted. When you have that two-way respect, with the guys who are sitting at the front of the bus scoring all the goals knowing that their success hinges on the guy playing seven minutes, I think that's a huge key to a closely knit team. They not only respect but count on those players to be an integral part of the game.

How do teams build and maintain trust?

That's a critical component because I have to trust that all players are on the same page and governed by the same rules. One of the breakdowns I've seen on teams I've played with happens when different guys have different rules to play under. From a trust factor it eats, it's like a cancer. It starts to eat away at the foundation of your team. You may have success during the regular season, but I can guarantee you it will come back to haunt you when the games get tougher and more critical. You may not even get away with it during the regular season because it may start to eat away at things more quickly and you'll have real trouble spots. I would be willing to bet that when the chips are down and things get tough in the playoffs, that's the thing that's going to break you down. There is a fine line, but a key component of any good team is that the top guy has the same set of rules as the bottom guy.

When you say "set of rules," what do you mean?

I don't mean rules as rules that are on the board, like you have to be in by 11:00. I mean the rules of your foundation of the game: how your team approaches and expects to win every night, how your team is going to break the puck out, how your team is going to do things in the neutral zone, how your team is going to defend in the neutral zone. If you're not on the same page, if the right winger isn't doing his job and the right defenceman gets exposed, that's the trust factor. Now you've got a situation where that right defenceman doesn't do his job, and so it starts to slowly erode away at your foundation of winning. That's what I mean by rules.

So, if you've got a couple of players who don't get along, can your team still function at a high level?

Absolutely, because I believe there's got to be an element of respect there. I may not go for dinner or hang out or spend time with him, but if I walk into a room and respect the job that the guy beside me is doing that is all that should matter. It's very seldom that you're going to put 23 guys together and every guy is going to get along well. That's great if it happens, but if it doesn't, when they walk in the room and look across and know and respect the job that every guy does, that's all that should really matter.

Describe a great team player for us.

A great team player is someone who is willing to sacrifice personal gain or goals for the betterment of the group. That's the guy who, instead of taking a shot at the open net, is going to make the safe play off the wall and scratch and claw at the red line to preserve the 4–3 win. That's a team player. Or, it's the guy on the number-one power play who, when things aren't going well, is saying, "I know I've got guys on the number-two power play that are very capable," so he doesn't overstay his shift. That's a team player. A team player is someone who is focused on one thing, team success, and is willing to sacrifice individual success, glory, or whatever, for the good of the team.

What did you do to become a great team player? How did you develop?

I felt that if the team had success, individuals would be successful. I've seen teams where individuals have great seasons, but it's with the cloud of missing the playoffs. No one really takes note, but when a team has a great year, a lot of those individuals are looked upon as having done great things, whether in the checking role, the penalty-killing role, the scoring role, or the defensive role. Everyone looks better when the team wins. I've often said that we can win 2–1 one night and everyone will say, "Wow, he did a lot of great things," and I can play exactly the same game and lose 2–1 the next night and they say I didn't do enough to win. That's a fair comment and proof to me that if you win, individual success will be there.

Who was your idol as a young player? Who influenced you the most?

As a young kid in Medicine Hat, I always looked up to Lanny MacDonald. He was a favourite of mine because he played in Medicine Hat, and I always admired (and this came largely from my parents) how he acted off the ice. It wasn't that he was the best player in the National Hockey League. I identified with him because he seemed like a good guy.

When I became a pro, I looked up to a guy like Bob Gainey, whom I was able to meet a few times in my career. I think even in your first years of pro you look at certain guys you come in contact with, like Bob, and another was Doug Wilson, and you say, "That's a guy I want to be like when I grow up." You would never think I could be 22 years old playing in the National Hockey League and wanting to be like my peers, guys that I played with and played against. I will never forget a story about leadership and Bob Gainey. He was the type of guy who never said much at all, but when he spoke in the locker room, there was complete silence. I think Jyrki Lumme told me that. Sitting down with Bob and having the good fortune of meeting him just on chance occasions, he is certainly someone I respect.

Who influenced your professional hockey development?

My parents were not really knowledgeable about hockey when I was a kid, which is probably a good thing. They were very supportive and always told me, "Good game," and it didn't matter if it was a good game or a bad game, which in hindsight was probably a good thing. Russ Farwell, who was the

GM of the Medicine Hat Tigers when I was a kid, was pretty influential. Even my minor hockey league coaches were helpful, and certainly when I got to junior I tried to learn as much as I could. Pat Quinn probably was the biggest influence on me. I was 20 years old when Pat coached me in Vancouver, and he taught me a lot. He's a great teacher.

How did you handle school and sport?

It wasn't tough for me because I made a pledge to my mother that if I played junior hockey, I had to graduate. I made that commitment and went to summer school that year to take some classes, because I knew that playing junior was a big commitment and I didn't want a full load of classes the next season. I sat on the bus many a night reading, working on whatever I had to do, and after the season I had a tutor. Both years I went to the Memorial Cup. I think that is a commitment not unlike your commitment to training in the summer or to working hard in practice. It all goes hand in hand. If you're going to take the easy way out when it comes to school work, chances are you'll take the easy way out when it comes to training or even playing. That was important for my parents.

If you could perform in any other occupation outside of hockey, what would it be and why?

I think I would be a farmer or a rancher because I like that style of work. I had the fortune of working for my uncle and my parents on the farm. It's a pretty simple life, pretty hard-working. I don't know if I would be any good at it, but I like that lifestyle.

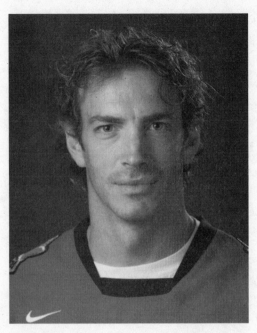

Joe Sakic

Although he was born in Vancouver, "Burnaby Joe" was officially claimed by the town he grew up in when the City of Burnaby named "Sakic Street" in his honour. After becoming a WHL All-Star and Rookie of the Year with the Swift Current Broncos in 1987, Joe Sakic was selected by the Quebec Nordiques in the first round of the draft, but he chose to return to the Swift Current Broncos after the first few days of his first NHL training camp. His decision paid off when Sakic played a key role in Team Canada's World Junior Championship gold medal win, won the WHL scoring title and the league MVP with 78 goals and 160 points in 64 games, was named to the WHL East First All-Star Team, and was named Canadian Major Junior Player of the Year by the time the 1987–88 season was complete.

When he made his NHL debut in 1988–89, Joe Sakic scored 62 points and co-led all rookies with 10 power-play goals. He was named captain as a sophomore in 1989–90, played in the all-star game and finished the season in the top 10 in scoring, with 102 points. In 1990–91 Sakic continued to improve, coming sixth in the league with 109 points.

Joe had his best offensive season, however, scoring 120 points, in 1995–96 when the Nordiques moved to Colorado and became the Avalanche. In the post-season he led the league with 34 points, scoring a spectacular NHL-record-setting 6 game-winning goals, including 2 in overtime, for a total of 18, the second-largest number in NHL playoff history and good enough to earn him the Conn Smythe Trophy and his team its first Stanley Cup. In 2001, he tied for the Bud Light Plus/Minus Award, and won the Lester B. Pearson, Lady Byng, and Hart Memorial trophies, while leading his team to its second Stanley Cup.

His international play has been equally impressive. Sakic played for Canada in the 1998 Nagano Olympics, the World Championships in Finland in 1991 and again in 1993 when Canada won its first gold medal since 1961. In 2002 Sakic, playing in his second Winter Olympics, helped Team Canada win its first gold medal in 52 years and was named MVP and to the All-Star Team in the process. In 2004 he was part of Canada's World Cup of Hockey victory and played yet again for Team Canada in the 2006 Winter Olympics.

Joe Sakic's personal accomplishments continue to impress. He passed Peter Stastny for first place on the Avalanche career-scoring list during the 1999–2000 season and is the all-time franchise leader in goals, assists, and points. He led his team in scoring for 6 straight seasons from 1989 to 1996 and again in 2001. He was named to the NHL First All-Star Team in 2001, 2002, and 2004, and played in the NHL All-Star Games in 1990, 1991, 1992, 1993, 1994, 1996, 1998, 2000, 2001, 2002, and 2004, when he was named MVP. He has scored 50 goals in two separate seasons and earned at least 100 points in six different seasons. On July 3, 2006, Sakic became the league leader for most NHL career points scored among active players. In 2007 he became the NHL's ninth all-time points leader, 14th in all-time goals, and 11th in all-time assists. On October 15, 2007, Joe Sakic was awarded the NHL Foundation Player Award in recognition of his charitable service.

In 2007, at age 37, Joe Sakic became the second-oldest NHL player to score 100 points in a season. The first was Gordie Howe. Not only has

Joe Sakic been an MVP in the Stanley Cup playoffs and the Most Valuable Player of a gold-medal-winning Team Canada at the Olympics, but he also played hockey on the silver screen with a cameo appearance in 1996's *Happy Gilmore*. Joe Sakic Hat Trick anyone?

The Interview

What were the qualities of some of the best leaders you ever played with?

I would have to start with Peter Stastny. When I broke into the league, I was in awe of him, as well as players like Michel Goulet. I remember when Peter came to the rink he was all business, and he said what he needed to say. He had so much respect from that dressing room. People listened to anything he said and took it in. He also played the game hard. If you tried to run him you couldn't. He would run over everybody. That's the way he was on the ice. He was a two-way player who worked hard every day. He was unbelievable in faceoffs, too. I was lucky to play with him and be able to see the way he acted. He was somebody to watch and learn from. He was only there for a year because the Quebec Nordiques started rebuilding after that, so I was fortunate to have had some time with him. A lot of guys don't have that opportunity. Easy learning, that's what that is.

So was Peter a leader?

For my game, yes, because I was at an impressionable age, where I was just starting my career. I don't think I could have found a better person both on and off the ice.

Would you say Peter had a presence about him?

Yes, he got respect from everybody.

How did he do that?

I am not sure. I think it was the way he conducted himself as a classy man on and off the ice—and what a hockey player.

What are your strongest leadership qualities?

I try to lead on the ice by working hard all the time. I try to be in the gym every morning. Off the ice, I'm pretty quiet. I like to have fun with the guys and joke around and things like that, but I don't say much unless I think there's something that has to be said. You hope you don't ever need to, but two or three times a year you inevitably need to do something.

How long have you worn the "C?"

I was officially named the captain of the Nordiques in 1992. Prior to that, we rotated the captaincy.

Have you felt pressure from having that "C?"

No, and I never have, right from the start. I always thought, "All right, I'm the captain, it's an honour," but I never felt pressure. Wearing the "C" didn't change my game at all. I was always going to try to do the same thing whether I had it or not.

In that context, Joe, how important is leadership within a professional hockey team room?

First of all, the more leaders you have the better off you are. I think the younger your team is, the better the leadership from the older guys needs to be. When kids come into the league they're impressionable, and the older guys lead the way. The kids are going to follow. If you have an older group, your team pretty much knows what they're doing, but it all depends on your team makeup.

How important are players who don't wear an "A" or a "C," the so-called glue guys that lead from the peripheral?

Huge—obviously, on the ice you want everybody to work hard and do whatever it takes to win, but off the ice you really need those guys. They do most of the talking, anyways. When I went to World Cups and Olympics and Mario Lemieux was there, he'd say whatever needed to be said, but it wasn't much. The role players did most of the talking. Everybody's really important to a team's success, but the role players do most of the talking. One guy who loves to talk is Ray Bourque. When he was with us in Colorado, he and Dave Reid both did a lot of talking, but before the games Ray would really get into it.

What do you respect about the coaches you've played for? Could you zoom in on a couple of them for us?

I'm pretty lucky. I've had a lot of great coaches, like Marc Crawford, especially once we got here to Colorado. As a bench coach there aren't too many better than Crow at reading the players and seeing who is going and getting the guys out there. I know with him that if you were going that night you were going to get more ice time than normal. Bob Hartley was great at the Xs and Os, the technical side of the game, and also the in-game match-ups. Joel Quenneville was kind of a combination. Every coach has had his unique style.

How do coaches get the best out of you?

I just try to be at my best all the time. I play hard and work hard all the time. There are some guys you can yell at and some guys you have to pat on the back. I guess that's what makes a good coach. You've got to see who to go after and find different ways to get them going, but you'd have to ask the coaches how to get me going. I try to play the same way all the time.

How much of motivating the player is the coach's job, or should motivation come more from the player's initiative?

If you ask me, it should all come from the players. The coaches shouldn't have to motivate us. We're playing a game, a game we've played since we were kids, and we shouldn't need extra motivation. But there are some games that are going to be tougher to get up for than other games, and each coach has a different way of trying to light a spark. It all depends on your team and who you're playing against. When you're playing 82 games, every game isn't going to be a Stanley Cup playoff game. In your last 15 games the coaches shouldn't have to say anything. You just look at the standings.

How do you like coaches to communicate to you?

Just really be honest and just talk. If there is something that they want me to do, they should just be honest and tell me what they're thinking. They shouldn't beat around the bush. If they treat you that way you are always going to have a great relationship with them.

Is it up to the coach to know how to communicate with his players?

I think as coaches get to know the players they learn that. Obviously it's harder if you just made a trade; then it will take some time for players and coaches to get to know each other. Every coach I've had has always done a good job of knowing how to communicate to different players.

What do you do as a player to create a winning environment?

A winning environment happens when you know everyone is on the same page and everybody is out for the same goal. That stems from the dressing room and the leadership. It's about your leaders and your role players all being on the same page. I've been pretty lucky. Since we've been here in Colorado we've pretty much had a winning environment every year, so I've kind of forgotten what it was like before. I know when you're in a winning environment you are confident and you go to the game expecting to win.

So expectation is a big part of it?

Expectation is a lot higher. When you're struggling, you're hoping to find a way to win rather than expecting to win. I think there's a big difference.

How do players impact this environment positively and negatively?

I think it's just body language, really. If you're on a good team, I don't know how you expect to win. It's just there. It's just one of those things.

Have you ever had a bad apple who's really affected the winning environment?

Actually, in Colorado, no. Anytime there was a bad apple, he wouldn't be around long. I think when you're in a winning environment there's less chance to have a bad apple because it's all about winning. But if you're in a losing environment it's easier to become a bad apple.

What motivates you?

The thrill of winning; there's nothing like it. I love playing the game. I love competing. I'm also motivated by the fear of losing, but in a good way. You get in those big games and you're excited, but some of my best games were when I had a bit of fear going into the game. I don't know how different guys react to it, but fear just makes me sharper.

What's the fear of, when you're really on?

Personally, just the fear of not playing well or making mistakes, but I guess some guys react differently. I don't know if fear is the right word for that feeling, but when I'm in it I focus more.

So if I say this, and it's kind of a hockey word, that we're "hungry," what does that mean to you?

To me it means you've got to be hungry to beat the other team. You want to win the battles on the puck. You want to be first to the puck.

How do you create team hunger?

I think you've got to have that makeup. It's really the makeup of your team that creates it.

How do you prepare to be your best, to play your best games? What do you do to prepare for a Stanley Cup final game?

You know what? I do the same thing every game day. It doesn't matter if it's a regular season game or a playoff game. I go to the rink in the morning, whether we skate or not, go back and have a pre-game meal, have a nap and go back to the rink. I do the same thing.

Do you visualize, Joe?

No, usually I don't think about the game at all during the day. I just try to relax, and then on the way to the game I'll think about it a little bit. When I get to the rink I'll tape sticks, I'll do laces, and I'll start thinking about the game at that point. Then again, if it's a playoff game in the Stanley Cup, I'll have the butterflies in the afternoon. I probably think about the game a little bit more if it's a playoff game, it's just human nature, but my routine doesn't change.

How did you develop your mental toughness?

I think you just learn the older you get. It starts coming after you've been around for awhile. It's a lot easier now to become focused than it was when I was younger. It's easier as you mature.

What is confidence and why is it so hard to put a finger on?

It depends on what position you play and your role. If you're a goalie it's probably different than if you are a scorer. If you're playing well, it seems you don't have to work as hard and you relax more. But when you're not confident and things aren't going well, it seems that the harder you work the harder it is to get anything done. Every player goes through it, that's not going to change. It's just when you have confidence you're a lot more relaxed, and it seems a lot less work than if you're struggling. It's tough going through it, but you're going to come out of it. The older you are, the more times you've been through losing confidence, and you just know you're going to come out of it.

Can the coach help or hinder your confidence?

Definitely. If things aren't going well and then your ice time drops, that's not going to help. But if the coach keeps putting you out there when it's not going well, and he shows that he believes in you, then you are going to come out of it quicker.

Tell us about a time that was an exciting moment for you when you were confident, when it was your best moment. Walk us through that.

I know one thing: in any game if you get off to a good start it makes a world of difference. You just relax and feel better. I think any player will tell you if you get off to a good start early on, it makes the rest of the night go a lot easier. Paul Kariya would always say, "You don't get going until your legs get going." I have thought about that and it's true.

How important is character to being a high-performance player?

I think it depends how you define it, but I know team-wise you're going to go through highs and lows, and if you've got a team with great character guys, you're going to get out of the lows a lot quicker than if you don't. To avoid distractions, you've got to understand you're going to go through all this and get out of it a lot quicker if you have the great character guys in the dressing room. Once you start going on a snowball downward, it's hard to get out of it, and if you don't have those strong character guys it's going to be tougher.

How do you personally get out of slumps?

They're not easy. I went 16 games without a goal right before the Salt Lake Olympics or before the All-Star Game that year. It didn't matter what I did, it wasn't going in. I was squeezing my stick. You keep trying to play well and trying to get out of the slump, but it's going to wear on you. It's funny, early in the first period I had a shot that I thought was in and the goalie saved it. I thought, "This is never going to happen," and then the next period our defenceman shoots it and it goes off my chest and into the net. That broke the slump, and then two minutes later I got another goal. It's hard to explain it when you're in it, but it's very frustrating. You've just got to stay with it.

How about off the ice, Joe? We all go through setbacks. How do you rebound from setbacks off the ice?

I think whatever you do, you've just got to find a way to relax and not worry. There is a tendency to worry a lot, and you've just got to find a way not to. Because I'm a hockey player and most of my tough times come from playing hockey, when I get home I leave the game at the rink. I try not to think about it. I have a wife and three kids, so it's a lot easier for me than somebody who's single. It's natural they would think about hockey more.

What were some of the difficult situations that you had to deal with as a young athlete, and how did you learn from them?

We did have a tough time in Swift Current when we lost four teammates when the bus crashed. It's really tough to go through a situation like that, but I think time heals everything. But when you're going through it you don't think like that.

Would you tell a young athlete that perseverance is important to a pro career?

Yes, because it's not always going to go smoothly, especially when you're young. The older and more experienced you become, the more you realize that you're going to need to persevere. When you're just starting out as a hockey player you don't see it as much because you're usually successful, but once the playing field levels out you won't have as many options as you did in minor hockey. This is something you have to learn to deal with. You've got to understand that you have to keep working and doing the same thing, and you have to take advice from the older guys who have been through it.

How do you build and maintain trust on a team?

First of all, winning definitely helps. That's the easiest way. Chemistry is a funny thing. It's difficult to define. For some reason or another you have chemistry with some line mates and you have a tougher time finding it with others. I think if everyone is on the same page and doing the same thing it makes it a lot easier, but there are those teammates like Kurri and Gretzky, Trottier and Bossy, for some reason they just click. You don't know why, but they are probably both thinking the same thing, the same way.

Can you tell someone outside of hockey what it means to be on the same page?

If you are thinking in hockey terms, you are thinking about what you're going to do in the play. You read what the other guy is thinking. If you've got a 2 on 2 you know what the puck carrier wants to do, and he knows what the other guy is going to do. It's anticipation, I guess.

Have you found over the years that teams that have chemistry all get along, or do they have to work through things?

For the most part I think teams who have chemistry do get along. You're not always going to agree on a team of 20 people. You don't expect everybody to agree on every little thing, but once you're on the ice everybody has the same goal. With the good chemistry, good character teams, when you get on the ice you're a team and you all stick together.

Red Fisher of Montreal once said there is no confidence. You either play well or you don't. What do you think?

It's a lot easier to play well when you have confidence. It is tough to talk about stuff like that with people who haven't played. Anybody who has played sports knows confidence. If you play golf it's the same thing. If you have confidence you'll play well. If you don't you're going to think about your swing.

How important is perseverance to you as a professional hockey player and to your team?

Perseverance is what goes on when you're facing adversity. You cannot sway or change. You know the right way, and you've got to keep doing it, keep battling through it. I guess there's a tendency to give up and just kind of slump down and maybe change the way you're doing something rather than continue doing the things that you know are successful but might not be working. You've got to just keep at it.

When the pressure is on, do you need to get more relaxed? Is that true of perseverance?

It depends how you use the word "relax." I think that perseverance is really fighting through and doing what you know is right, what you know you have to do and never swaying from that. Keep doing it until it comes. You don't quit, you just keep fighting through it. Whether it's personal or team-related you just keep going. You don't stop.

What qualities do you look for in a closely knit team?

Team-wise it is everybody having the same goal in mind. You're going to have different personalities on a team, but when you're on the ice, every team has a team philosophy and everybody's sticking to it. On the personal side, you've got guys who click and have that chemistry with certain guys and maybe not with others, but team-wise a closely knit team requires everybody being on the same page and sticking to it by following the team philosophy.

So within this closely knit team is trust a big issue?

Trust is everything. If a defenceman doesn't trust a forward on a backcheck, he'll play that a little differently than if he knows the forward's going to be back in the same position. If he trusts the forward, he doesn't have to worry, he can just play. But if he doesn't have that trust in the forward to be there, then he might not be as aggressive on the puck. Trust is everything on a team.

How do you build and maintain trust?

You don't have trust right away. You have to build it over the course of the year. If everyone is on the same program and doing the right things that certainly speeds up the process. Everyone should be playing the same defensively. Offensively you are going to have your Forsberg-type players who have more flexibility and creativity, but to build trust it is important for the team to stick to a set structure. As the season goes on and the guys buy in, you are going to develop that trust.

What are the ingredients of a great team player?

A great team player to me is someone who accepts his role. It is important that everyone accepts their role. Let's say someone gets traded and he had a certain role on one team and then he goes to a different team and his role changes. He might be playing with different guys. I think accepting that and always being positive and buying into the team program is being a team player.

Do you think about doing specific things to become a team player, or is it an evolution through junior and into professional hockey?

It's a lot easier when you're on a good team. It's tougher if you're struggling. I'm not saying everybody, but some people's tendencies are to kind of sway from what is good for the team, if the team is not doing well, and individually do something different. It's a lot easier to be a team player on a good team because you're having fun. Back in the early days in Quebec we were a young team, and, as we have discussed about leadership, if you don't have the guys to show you the way it can be harder for a younger guy on an already young team. If you are on an established team it's easier to fit in.

What would you say about being a team player to a young junior player on a struggling team who reads this book?

Your coaches have a system, and I think you just have to buy into the system and work within the team framework. You do what you're asked to do. I am thinking the team stuff is more on the defensive side of the game, your play without the puck. Offensively, to me, it's a different thing. The coaches know everybody has different abilities with the puck so there may be some variance in how guys play, but away from the puck, if you can get everybody doing the same thing it's going to make it a lot easier. An example of that is playing with the score. If you're up a couple of goals with five minutes left in the game, you always want to play the same way defensively, but you also want to make sure you aren't doing anything offensively to put your team in jeopardy, like turning the puck over at the blue line. A team player will play it smart and get the puck in deep. He won't cheat to score. He will play on the defensive side rather than the offensive side of the puck. Playing the score is another big way of being a team player. You have to know how to play in certain situations.

So you're reliable because you're putting the team first?

And you're not always taught that. You can tell if a guy is playing within the team structure. Doing that makes a big difference, especially amongst your peers. If your teammate sees a top offensive player maybe chipping the puck in if it's a 1 on 2 and then changing, and staying on the defensive side rather than cheating to the offensive side, that really shows that he is a team player.

Can you put an umbrella over the culmination of what a team player really is, all those little pieces?

Everybody's objective is to succeed, and the only way to succeed in a team sport is when the team does it together.

Mike Johnston holds a master's degree in Coaching Science. He began his head-coaching career at Camrose Lutheran College in 1982 and then moved to the University of New Brunswick, where he compiled three consecutive first-place finishes and two McAdam Division titles from 1989 to 1994. He won the Saint-John *Telegraph-Journal* Coach of the Year award in 1993, and was named 3M Coach of the Year in 1994.

Mike guided Canada to two World Junior Championships as an assistant coach and won three Spengler Cup gold medals coaching the Team Canada Selects. He won bronze and silver medals with Canada's National Team at the 1995 and 1996 World Championships and a gold medal in 1997. After four seasons as assistant coach with the Canadian National Team, he became head coach and GM in 1998 as well as assistant coach for Team Canada at the 1998 Winter Olympics. He was invited to coach in the 2007 World Championship, where Canada again won gold.

As associate coach from 1999 to 2006, Mike played a major developmental role in the Vancouver Canucks' consecutive 100-points-plus seasons and subsequent Northwest Division championship in 2004. He joined the LA Kings coaching staff in 2006.

Ryan Walter played more than 1,000 games over 15 seasons in the NHL. Drafted second overall by the Washington Capitals in 1978, Ryan became the youngest NHL captain in his second of four seasons, went on to win a Stanley Cup during his nine seasons with the Montreal Canadiens and finished his career as an assistant captain with his hometown team, the Vancouver Canucks. He captained Team Canada in the World Junior tournament, played in the NHL All-Star game and for Team Canada in four World Championships, was a vice-president of the NHLPA and was honoured as NHL Man of the Year.

Ryan is both an inspiring motivational speaker and an interactive leadership coach whose mission is to inspire the hungry spirit. He has a Master of Arts in Leadership/ Business, co-founded two start-up companies, and is the author of two books. *Off the Bench and Into the Game*, now updated and expanded, has sold over 20,000 copies worldwide and is available at www.ryanwalter.com along with Ryan's original board game *Trade Deadline Hockey*. Ryan is a television hockey analyst, is in the reality-TV series *Making the Cut* and the animated TV show *Being Ian* and plays an expert adviser and actor in the movie *Miracle*. **Book Ryan to inspire your corporation or team at 1-866-728-3603 or www.ryanwalter.com.**

Also by Ryan Walter

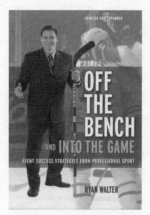

Off the Bench and Into the Game
Eight Success Strategies from Professional Sport
Updated and expanded

ISBN 13: 978-1-894974-23-3
ISBN 10: 1-894974-23-9

Our lives are in a constant state of change. We move from times of extreme confidence and accelerated performance to times of disappointment and discouragement. As the speed of life increases, we sometimes feel like we are wasting our potential, sitting on the bench rather than achieving success by flying down the ice.

In this revised, updated and expanded edition of his inspirational book, Ryan Walter explores performance and success, using techniques he learned during 15 years in the NHL. His subjects range from mental toughness and successful habits of thought to leadership and the differences between being a player, a team player and a leader.

"Ryan's ability to separate the important from the trivial, and support it with clear, easy-to-understand life experiences, is just marvelous."

—Bob Gainey, executive vice-president and general manager, Montreal Canadiens

"Ryan Walter's book is a must-read for any executive inside or outside of sport. This is a critically useful tool for any athlete who is trying to maximize his or her athletic ability. Finally, this is an inspirational read for any young person trying to sort things out."

—Brian Burke, executive vice-president and general manager, Anaheim Ducks

Also by Mike Johnston and Ryan Walter

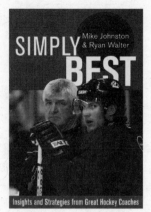

Simply the Best
Insights and Strategies
from Great Hockey Coaches
Second Edition

ISBN 978-1-894974-37-0

Scotty Bowman • Marc Crawford • Jacques Demers • Clare Drake • Ken Hitchcock • Mike Keenan • Dave King • George Kingston • Andy Murray • Roger Neilson • Pat Quinn • Brian Sutter

Simply the Best delivers rare insights on success straight from the hearts and minds of winning coaches. These world-renowned hockey visionaries, recognized as some of the greatest coaches in the game, discuss in their own words what it takes to be a champion and the strategies that have made them successful.

Each one of us is a coach, whether we are raising children, coaching a youth sports team, being the project team leader at work, teaching students in a classroom or managing employees in a corporation. *Simply the Best* makes it clear that these coaches' mastered principles of success are also relevant off the ice, so that people in all walks of life can win their own Stanley Cups.

"I was recently directed to your book by a friend, and I have to say it's been incredibly eye-opening to me ... many thanks for a great, inspirational book."

—Bill Driscoll, director/head coach, North American Hockey Academy